WINNING
CONDITIONS

WINNING
CONDITIONS

How to Achieve the Professional Success You
Deserve by Managing the Details That Matter

CHRISTINE HOFBECK

V!VA
EDITIONS

Published in the United States by Viva Editions, an imprint of Start Midnight, LLC, 221 River Street, Ninth Floor, Hoboken, NJ 07030.

Printed in the United States.
Cover design: Jennifer Do
Cover image: Shutterstock
Text design: Frank Wiedemann

First Edition.
10 9 8 7 6 5 4 3 2 1
Trade paper ISBN: 978-1-63228-070-1
E-book ISBN: 978-1-63228-126-5

Quotes from *Survivor*, season 35, episode 14, "Million Dollar Night," used with permission.

Some names and identifying details have been changed to protect personal privacy.

For Keith,
You are still
and have always been
my everything.

And for everyone who knows
they have greatness inside
and now is ready
for the rest of the world to see it too.

TABLE OF CONTENTS

MY WINNING STORY

wasn't born a winner. There was a time when I came up just short of success in seemingly everything I tried. In high school I tried out for the field hockey team and made the bench. I worked hard at every practice, but I never played a single minute of any game the entire season. I tried out for the school play and made the chorus. The way, way in the tippy back chorus where no one in the audience could either see me or hear me. I ran for senior class president and lost the election to Janice Dewey, a popular and pretty girl who seemed to have far less interest in the position than I did. I spent the summer before my senior year reading the required thousand-page *Gone With the Wind* for my honors English class and agonized for weeks over the essay. My best friend, Holly, watched the movie on the last day of summer and knocked out that essay in two hours flat. She got an A. I got a B. Holly was remarkable. I was decidedly unremarkable. But I was headed off to college, where I was determined to be something.

And then in college, it all changed.

I started to become aware of something I characterized as "winning conditions"—a framework in which I could actually control the conditions around the delivery of my efforts to notably improve my outcomes. I began to recognize that success isn't necessarily built *only* on the work or effort itself. It isn't necessarily and automatically based on who is the smartest, or who works the longest, or who has the best skills or the most focused résumé or the most innovative ideas. Often, success can also be influenced by the manner in which you share or present your work or effort. Small improvements in delivery could result in substantial improvements in outcome. I started to realize that with the right conditions in place, just maybe I could begin to win.

Now, this consideration of winning conditions wasn't a conscious realization at the time. It began instead as a feeling, a seed, an unformed idea that first took hold after a curious experience that proves either my dogged persistence or my penchant for punishment: senior class elections. You'd think after the Janice Dewey incident I might have tried something else, but four years had elapsed since the high school debacle, and by my junior year in college, I felt like I had finally found myself. Sure, in high school I was awkward and nerdy and relentlessly made fun of. Every. Single. Day. But college was different for me. College was joyful and accepting. It was academically challenging and a safe place to flourish. It was the first time in my life that I fit in. I had friends—so many friends. People used to say that between my friend Debra and myself, we knew the entire school.

I thrived. There was so much to do. When I wasn't in class or doing homework, I was playing cards with my housemates (so many card games) or working (catering and bartending) or going to parties (too many parties) or tutoring (math and German) or volunteering (children's cancer research was our charity of choice) or exploring (downtown Philly, the art museum, the Franklin Institute) or studying (for the actuarial exams that I was already conquering on my own). There was always something. When there was nothing, I'd go be a guinea pig for the psych student experiments or sit in the sun on College Green. I never wanted this to end.

But I was coming up on the end of my junior year at Penn, and I knew it would end too soon. One day I was talking with a senior who told me that the president of the senior class carries the American flag during the graduation processional, and the vice president of the class carries the Penn flag. That's all I needed to hear. I wanted to carry the Penn flag on behalf of my graduating class and close out my college career celebrating the place that made me whole. I had no business running for the VP position. I had no experience in student government while at college and hadn't taken on any leadership positions in any other groups on campus. I hadn't even held the position in high school—remember, those were the Janice Dewey days. But despite all that, I decided that I was going to make a run for it.

I remember finding out that I was running against my classmate James. James was prelaw and had been involved in student government groups and panels every year since freshman year. Senior class vice president was a natural progression for him. He ran a strong campaign. They all told me I'd never beat him, because James had everything going for him. James was going to win, he was poised to win, he was the obvious choice to win.

Except he didn't. Because I did.

It turns out, I had everything going for me. Well, maybe not everything, but it seems I had the details that mattered. Perhaps it was that I knew the right people and had the right support. Perhaps I had created enough rich experiences during my time at Penn that the students felt connected to me. Maybe it was because I had done a good job promoting my own value during the election cycle. Whatever it was, I had unknowingly stumbled into the right winning conditions for this particular experience. I might not have had as strong a résumé as James, but I delivered my election pitch and positioned my candidacy in a winning way. I was able to influence my outcome in a winning way. For the first time in as long as I could remember, I had gone after a dream . . . and won.

My time on the senior class board was extraordinary. We created countless experiences for our class, including launching a month-long event called the Feb Club, which later became a Penn tradition.

Leading my college graduation processional. Image courtesy of Kiera Reilly.

On graduation day, I led my graduating class down Locust Walk and onto Franklin Field while proudly carrying the Penn flag. I still consider that event to be one of the best things I've ever done in my entire life. I continued my service to my class as vice president and reunion cochair for twenty-seven years, and throughout those twenty-seven years, our class won multiple awards for excellence in leadership and event planning.

But winning that class board election did far more than greatly enrich my undergraduate and alumni experience. It also yielded a lifelong and highly important lesson: things that I thought were out of reach might actually be within reach if I could learn to create the right winning conditions. I began to believe that I could potentially leave those repeated failures behind. And I just might be capable of significantly more than I had previously thought possible.

After that election, I relentlessly pondered this experience. It didn't make a lot of sense. On paper, James should have beaten me.

He was the obvious choice to win. Back in high school, I should have beaten Janice. Why did these results play out the way they did? Why doesn't the "best" candidate or the "best" work always win? If you truly are the best, is there a way to ensure that your best does win? I thought about this constantly, almost to obsession. I pondered other life experiences beyond those elections. I could not stop thinking about this idea of winning conditions. I could not stop considering whether success and failure might go beyond the work or effort itself, and might also be influenced by the manner in which you share or present that work or effort. This idea seemed to permeate everything I did, and everything I wanted to do. I wondered:

▸ How often had I been the stronger candidate, with higher technical competency, more applicable training, or greater dedication, but I lost out to someone who simply delivered their work in a winning way?

▸ If I could begin to make even small improvements in the delivery of my own efforts, could I potentially affect substantial improvements in my outcomes? Could I do over and over what I had done in that election?

▸ If I could develop a more valuable approach or system for delivering my quality work, could I consistently increase my opportunity for success? Could I repeatedly leverage a winning conditions framework to more consistently achieve my goals?

▸ And could I be happier and more satisfied along the way?

After graduation and throughout the next three decades, I continued to research, test, and explore these ideas through multiple outlets. I worked my way through a rewarding actuarial career, from independent contributor to executive adviser for numerous large global companies. I ducked out of the business world for a while to enjoy wonderfully joyful years as a stay-at-home mom to my three great kids. I tackled graduate school and secured an MBA. I traveled through seven continents and volunteered extensively both at home and abroad. I competed in one of the most popular reality television games in history.

Along this journey, I took increasing notice of people succeeding not simply because they were delivering a winning work product or idea, but because *they were delivering their work in a winning way.* Over these three decades, I fed my natural curiosity about winning conditions by talking with countless people across industries, countries, levels, and roles about their experiences. I devoured books on persuasion and decision making, studied behavioral economics concepts in graduate school, and tested and proved my ideas in my own career. Consulting and volunteering provided rich opportunities to engage on countless projects with diverse teams in many different types of organizations. I became involved with their various strategies, perspectives, ideas, goals, problems, solutions, resources, and people. This myriad of experiences allowed me to compare and contrast, explore and dissect. And I did. Long gone were those earlier days of always just missing the mark. Because now, the more I tested my winning conditions framework, the more I won. I began to experience significant recognition and celebration of my work and my efforts. My business partners kept coming back to me for more.

As my career progressed, I was honored to be named a *pioneer* and a *trailblazer* in my male-dominated industry through multiple print and television outlets. I was invited to share my professional expertise in the critically acclaimed National Geographic Channel documentary series *Breakthrough.* I was admitted to graduate school at one of the most prestigious schools in the country—the Massachusetts Institute of Technology. After sixteen years of submitting applications, I was finally selected to play CBS's *Survivor*—and placed on a starting team designated the Heroes. *Survivor*'s host and executive producer, Jeff Probst, labeled me a hero because, in his words, I "broke the glass ceiling in terms of business."[1] I was elected to the board of directors of the Society of Actuaries and began guest lecturing at top universities and events, eventually becoming an in-demand speaker both at home and abroad.

It turns out, I was indeed capable of significantly more than I had previously thought possible. Because once I learned how to develop and embrace my winning conditions, I could create and live my own winning story.

YOU CAN DO IT TOO

The framework that I will present to you in this book is simple, but it will change your life for the better. Stop for a moment to think about the experiences that you have had in your life.

▸ Do you ever see people who are perhaps not as smart, dedicated, hardworking, or well trained as you are, but they seem to be more successful?

▸ Do you wish you could have the same amount of success . . . *or more*?

▸ Do you know you have great ideas but can't seem to get traction with them? Or you'd like more traction with them?

▸ Do you ever wish that when you shared your great ideas, you'd get a different (or better) reaction?

▸ Do you wish that your boss, your team, your partner, your [fill in the blank] would just listen to you about this one [or two, or more] thing(s)?

---

1 Wigler, Josh. "'Survivor' Season 35: Jeff Probst Previews the Heroes Tribe." *The Hollywood Reporter*, August 31, 2017. https://www.hollywoodreporter.com/live-feed/survivor-season-35-jeff-probst-previews-heroes-tribe-1032830

▶ Do you ever feel like you are finding it harder and harder
   to get ahead, while others seem to easily climb the corporate ladder or gain recognition?

▶ Do you wish it were that easy for you?

You CAN have all of this, and more. By fine-tuning the delivery of
your work, you can create your own winning story. Let me say that
again so you remember it well:

YOU CAN CREATE YOUR OWN WINNING STORY.

Let's face it: if you're taking the time to read this book, then I assume
you're already motivated to deliver high-quality work. So let's get
you to a place where you're winning this game every time—or at
least a lot of the time. Or more of the time! By implementing a more
valuable approach for delivering your great work, you can begin to
increase your opportunities for success, more consistently achieve
your goals, and be happier and more satisfied along the way. You,
too, can dream . . . and win.

What if you're just entering the workforce? What if you're
approaching retirement? What if you're an individual contributor,
or self-employed, or a volunteer? Can you still use these ideas? Yes.
Yes. Yes. These ideas can be used at any age, role, or situation. In
fact, you can even use them outside the workplace, in your own
personal interactions.

What does it even mean to "win"? Doesn't this mean different
things for different people? Yes, it does. A win may be gaining
traction, getting noticed, or being trusted. It may be receiving recognition for a job well done, getting a callback, or being considered for
a promotion. Maybe you are selected, or maybe you simply do better
than expected. Any of these may be a win. The options are vast and
most definitely personal. But always, the win in the context of this
book reflects a positive decision, view, or impression. So here, we're
not talking about how to win random games of chance (I won't be

providing tips on picking the right lotto numbers). We're also not talking about how to become technically stronger in your field (I won't be teaching engineers how to build a better widget). Instead, you'll learn how to manage the conditions around the *delivery* of your already quality work, so that your colleagues and the other people around you believe in you and your work and respond positively and optimally.

What if the situation you're in is "unwinnable"? Do winning conditions still apply? Yes—you can, and you should, still work to create your winning conditions. Even in seemingly unwinnable situations, the framework will help you to consistently achieve the best possible outcomes. For example, maybe, despite your best efforts, you are faced with workforce reductions and your position is eliminated. In this case, let's use these techniques to negotiate an extra few months of benefits and ace those upcoming interviews. Let's make such a positive impression that we can secure influential references and contacts for new opportunities. Okay, you have lost your job, but let's find a way to improve the outcome. Every situation— even the bad ones—can be improved through winning conditions.

This book will provide simple and easy methods that you can use to deliver your quality work, service, or ideas in ways that are more likely to be noticed, praised, and accepted. They will work for everyone regardless of role, level, or experience. And after you have read this book and you begin to *consciously* implement this simple and easy framework, you will see your colleagues and those around you respond more positively to your work. You will see improved outcomes. You will see your reputation and overall success improve.

You will begin to win.

THE FINE PRINT

As you embark on this journey toward winning conditions, I want to point out a few things. First, throughout this book, I will often use the terms "colleague" and "business partner" interchangeably. Because these terms may have different meanings in varied roles and industries, I'd like to briefly define them. In the context of this book, a "colleague" or a "business partner" means any person with whom you interact in the course of doing business. Your colleagues and business partners may be any level, tenure, role, or relationship to you, and may be internal or external to your organization. They could be your managers, direct reports, peers, vendors, clients, customers, or anyone else with whom you work. If you want to apply these concepts to your personal life, then they could be your friends, neighbors, family members, or community contacts. Please resist the urge to think of "colleagues" or "business partners" as only those of high status or of a necessarily corporate nature. Here, the summer intern is the business partner and colleague of the CEO.

Second, I often refer to "winning conditions" as a singular noun. That's because winning conditions is a global idea, a framework, a mindset, or a way of thinking. It's not a collection of various instructions that you'll need to meticulously study and memorize. I can assure you that by the end of this book, you'll be fully comfortable with the framework, and as you create or stumble upon the ideas in your own real experiences, you'll easily and proudly share, "This is winning conditions!"

Lastly, I've noticed over many years of reading and research that many nonfiction motivational or business books start with the foundational assumption that we are flawed. Those books are meant to help us, yet they start by pointing out all the things that we're doing wrong. They make a point of noting our mistakes. They assert that our poor decisions are limiting our impact and our success. We are placed at fault so the glorious author can dig us out of this mess we've made.

Not this one. I'm starting with the assumption that you are already outstanding. Maybe you don't know that right now, but I know it. You are outstanding. You are exceptional. You are working hard, and you are striving to better yourself. You are motivated and dedicated. You take pride in your work and all that you have to offer. The sky's the limit for you, if you want it. If you don't want it, well, then, whatever you want is the perfect decision for you. Your choices and opinions are valid and valuable.

Any issues that you may have are *not* because you are flawed, but because you are human. So, don't start this read from a place of fear. Start it from a place of joy. You can do this. You *will* do this. Let's show the world what you are capable of. Because I bet you are capable of significantly more than you ever thought possible.

With a spirit of joy and positivity, come join me. Let's go on a journey to create YOUR winning story.

Here we go.

PART 1:

EMBRACE THE BIGGER PICTURE

CHAPTER 1

DEVELOP YOUR CONSCIOUS AWARENESS

I am a prisoner of the extra-long commute. I love living in my little rural town, but unfortunately this means that my most meaningful job opportunities are often quite far away. I've never commuted less than an hour each way. One of my positions was four hours round trip. Four hours, ugh! I won't do that anymore, though, because there were a couple times during that commute when I found myself going into autopilot. Has this ever happened to you? Have you ever driven a particularly long route and unintentionally lost yourself in your own thoughts, so when you "woke up" it took a moment to figure out where you were? Maybe you weren't sure if you'd passed your exit or hadn't even reached it yet. This is called mindless driving, and it can be extremely dangerous. Drivers have been known to end up in another city or state after periods of mindless driving, or far worse. Please don't do this. I put an end to that four-hour commute so I could put an end to the potential for mindless driving.

But we do other things mindlessly as well. Have you ever mindlessly eaten an entire tub of ice cream while watching your favorite television show? Have you ever mindlessly put your keys down somewhere and then had no idea where they were? Have you ever forgotten whether you'd already taken out your contact lenses and had to actually rub your eyeball to find out? I've been known to madly search the house for my eyeglasses, not realizing that I mindlessly perched them on the top of my own head.

Sometimes we also do our work mindlessly. Perhaps we work a particular position or role so long that we begin to move into an autopilot state. We've done this precise task or job a million times already, so we don't think anymore as we execute it. Perhaps we're preoccupied with things at home, so we're less deliberate at work. The baby is sick, the mortgage is due, the basement flooded—each of these might be understandably taking up our active brain space and crowding out workplace thoughts during the workday. Sometimes we're just so tired from the endless grind that we survive by simply going through the motions. Our brains are maxed out, and we're exhausted. We don't have room for one more thing. All of these can—and do—happen to even the best of us.

Perhaps we're mindless for a different reason. Maybe we are truly working wholeheartedly, attentively, and deliberately, but we've accidentally overlooked some details that matter because we're focusing on different details. Our thoughtful brains just made an honest mistake. Just a few days ago I received a LinkedIn invitation from someone whose bio/headline told me they were "perusing a degree in mathematics." Now, I don't know them at all, but something tells me that they're probably *pursuing* a degree, not *perusing* a degree. They probably created their LinkedIn profile thoughtfully and carefully but just made a spelling error in the headline. Unfortunately, this small spelling error is the big difference between impressing their audience by sharing that they're going after something great with a strong determination ("pursuing") or boring their audience by suggesting they're unimpressively glancing over something without specific intent ("perusing"). Their unintentional error changed the entire context of the bio. And this example isn't even anything uncommon. I've more than once received thoughtfully crafted and detailed solicitations from job recruiters that are unfortunately addressed "Dear Jennifer" or any other name that is decidedly not Christine. I had a colleague who was once so worried about the talking points of a big presentation that they mistakenly forgot to send the attendees an updated invitation with the new meeting location. Nobody showed up.

Becoming more mindful in your work and in your life is a central component of winning conditions. In the introduction, I mentioned that you will begin seeing improved outcomes if you *consciously* implement the ideas in the framework. "Consciously" means that you are actively doing something in a deliberate, attentive, and thoughtful way. You are intentionally making improvements. You will become consciously aware. So let's explore this idea of conscious awareness a little bit. We'll establish the importance of conscious awareness by first exploring its opposing phenomenon, unintentional blindness.

UNINTENTIONAL BLINDNESS

The human brain is an incredible thing. Our incredible brains allow us to function, learn, remember, analyze, strategize, and feel. They allow us to think, care, consider, reflect, and reason. Our incredible brains also forget, err, mess up, and break down. Sometimes we humans are wholly impressive, and sometimes we are downright irrational. But curiously for us humans, often this irrationality is consistently predictable. This *predictable irrationality* is the basis of the science of behavior called *behavioral economics*.

Behavioral economics explores the many ways in which humans make irrational decisions—not because we're not smart, not hard-working, not motivated, not strategic, or not responsible, and definitely not because we don't care or because we're flawed—but instead because we're human and we possess human brains. This is science. Our brains, at times, predictably mess up in remarkably consistent ways. It happens to all of us. In fact, the next time you find yourself frustrated in a workplace interaction, remind yourself that whoever is frustrating you might be behaving that way simply because they are human and have a predictably irrational human brain—not because they are necessarily bad or intentionally trying to be frustrating.

One example of this predictable irrationality is that we can become "blind" to certain important things, simply because we focus on different important things. It's a phenomenon called *unintentional blindness* (or, sometimes, *inattentional blindness*), and it occurs when our brains are so focused on a particular task or subject that we fail to see something else, perhaps something unexpected, that is also happening right before our eyes. The phenomenon is thought to have developed more than two million years ago, at a time when humans needed to be laser focused on animals—both as predator and prey—in order to survive. And what began as a survival mechanism still exists today: our human attention system will sometimes completely ignore something if we're not specifically focusing on it.

This is what happens when we go into autopilot while driving a long route—we become blind to the drive as we instead concentrate on our own thoughts. This is what happens when we mindlessly eat a tub of ice cream while we're focused on enjoying our favorite television program. This is what happens when we forget to send an updated meeting invitation because we're obsessing over our talking points. Our human brains have fallen into a state of unintentional blindness. And remember, this happens not because we're lazy or irresponsible, but because we're human.

One of the most entertaining and well-known research examples of unintentional blindness was released by two professors, Drs. Christopher Chabris and Daniel Simons, in the late 1990s. They created a short video experiment in which the viewer is asked to count the number of times a basketball is passed within a small circle of people. In the middle of the video, a large gorilla (really a person in a gorilla suit) struts directly into the center of the circle, pounds its chest, and then exits. Remarkably, about half the people who watch the video don't even notice the gorilla. They're too busy focusing on the basketball.[2]

A few years ago, Colgate-Palmolive brilliantly leveraged our human tendency toward unintentional blindness in an advertising campaign for dental floss. In the series of images, the broadly smiling subject of the ad has a large and rather gross-looking piece of food stuck right in his front teeth. It's super distracting. It's so distracting, in fact, that the audience often doesn't realize that the only other person in the ad—the friend—has six fingers. In another version of the ad, the friend has three arms. In yet another version, the subject is missing an ear. Everyone better run out immediately and buy some dental floss—because food in your teeth is so distracting that you may not even notice major anatomical abnormalities!

What's interesting is that when the gorilla, extra finger, third arm, and missing ear are pointed out, they're incredibly obvious. How could you miss them? Of course you see them. Yet again and again, our human brains naturally fall into a pattern of unintentional blindness. Even when we think we're paying attention, there are details that we miss because we're concentrating on something else. This is normal. Winning conditions helps us to overcome this tendency. *Winning conditions* means learning to look for and find the details that matter. It means making small changes in your behavior based on these conscious observations in order to notably improve your outcomes.

> *Winning conditions means learning to look for and find the details that matter. It means making small changes in your behavior based on these conscious observations in order to notably improve your outcomes.*

Consider the following experience from my first job.

---

2 Chabris, Christopher, and Simons, Daniel. "The invisible gorilla." theinvisiblegorilla.com (accessed November 1, 2019).

OUT OF THE SHADOWS

Fort Lee, New Jersey, 1993. I had just graduated from the University of Pennsylvania and had begun my actuarial career at Kwasha Lipton, an employee benefits consulting firm. Kwasha was a great place to work because it was overflowing with outgoing, brilliant, creative, and positive consultants. I learned new technical skills every day. I learned how to program, how to process and understand complex regulations, and how to manage clients. I was simultaneously studying for my actuarial exams and learning about difficult mathematical and financial functions, theories, and markets. I was hyperaware of learning as much as I could, as fast as I could. I loved every second of this fast-paced, driven environment.

Our office had a distinct spirit of friendly competition, and within each cohort of new hires (the group of consultants who were hired out of university in the same year) there was a definite awareness of who had passed which actuarial exams, who had been promoted, and who was working with the biggest names and the most influential, or "best," clients. My cohort included a woman named Roselyn. Everybody loved Roselyn. She and I had similar backgrounds, passed exactly the same actuarial exams, and worked on all the best clients, yet everyone talked about the Amazing Roselyn. People didn't talk about the amazing christine (lowercase intended).

There was a television show in the 1970s called *The Brady Bunch*. I loved that show when I was a kid. It shared the lives of two parents, six kids, and a housekeeper. Anyway, in one of the episodes, middle sister Jan goes to high school and is frustrated that all her teachers just keep nonstop raving about her big sister, Marcia. "Marcia, Marcia, Marcia," they all say. And all this vocalized adoration makes middle sister Jan feel substandard. She feels invisible. Jan feels like she is constantly living in the shadow of her big sister, Marcia. In fact, the episode is titled "Her Sister's Shadow."

Well, this is exactly how I felt at work. Roselyn, Roselyn, Roselyn.

And yup, I'm Jan. I'm doing all I can, yet everybody just keeps raving about Roselyn. She and I were delivering the same results, innovations, and solutions, and yet somehow she was winning every time. Despite my excellent work, I was dependably living in Roselyn's shadow.

I wanted to change this. So instead of blindly accepting my shadow status, I consciously decided to try to figure out what she was doing right. I wanted to learn from Roselyn. Yes, I loved her, too. When I opened my eyes to consciously pay attention to the details, I recognized that Roselyn was delivering her work differently than I was. Same work—different delivery. The way that she interacted with our colleagues drove them to feel a particular way about her. She was setting up her own winning conditions. It was right there before my eyes, I just had never noticed it before.

Here's one simple example that made a strong impact on outcome. When Roselyn was complimented on her work, she graciously and thoughtfully said thank you. *"Roselyn, great job on those results!"*

> *Thank you, I worked really hard on the project.*
> *Thank you so much.*
> *Thanks, I really enjoyed working on the project.*

As you can imagine, Roselyn's managers learned from her response that she worked really hard. They learned that she enjoyed her work. These two bits of information led them continue to give her challenging and important work that she enjoyed.

When my work was praised, I responded differently. *"Christine, great job on those results!"*

> *Thanks, but it was really just a simple update.*
> *Thanks, but it really wasn't that big of a deal.*
> *Oh, it was easy—I just repeated what we did last year.*

I deflected. I guess I thought I was being humble, unpretentious, or discreet. My humble, unpretentious, discreet response became mindless and automatic. I just said it. Every time. *"Thanks, but it really wasn't that big of a deal."*

But repeated humility, while coming from a place of goodness, can ultimately lead to a decline in recognition. Over time, our colleagues will begin to think that the work we did was simple, or it wasn't that big of a deal, or it was easy to just repeat what we did last year. And they will think that because we told them so. They may stop praising us or recognizing our valuable contributions—because we ourselves have assured them that our contributions aren't actually all that valuable. We have made ourselves insignificant, and therefore, others may think of us as insignificant. Others didn't put us in the shadows—instead, we put ourselves there. When my colleagues expressed gratitude to me, I didn't accept it or receive their gratitude in a meaningful way.

Roselyn showed me that it is wholly possible to accept praise without sounding egotistical, arrogant, or narcissistic. It is possible to respond in a way that inspires warmth and satisfaction and security. It is possible to graciously shine a light on our accomplishments—and ourselves. In reality, she did work really hard on that project. She did enjoy the work. Her responses did not undermine others. She accepted compliments appropriately and with great poise. She honored the work and the process. She honored the praise and the praiser without dismissal.

Thank you, I worked really hard on the project.
Thank you so much.
Thanks, I really enjoyed working on the project.

But I didn't naturally see this until I *consciously* decided to look.

Roselyn and I worked with others who were on the "no problem" bandwagon. Do you know people who ride this ride? *"Joe, great job on those results!"*

No problem.

But there actually is a problem here, and Joe himself unintentionally and mindlessly introduced it. To explain the problem, we need to first understand yet another phenomenon of our human brains. That is, a human brain is physically unable to ignore something that has been brought to its attention. This is sort of the complement of unintentional blindness. In unintentional blindness, we might accidentally ignore something that we *don't* specifically focus on. Here, we cannot ignore something that we *do* specifically focus on. For example, if I tell you that my desk chair is wrapped in cotton candy, then you probably just thought about a desk chair and/or cotton candy. Why? Because you have a human brain, and so when I brought the idea to your attention, you were simply unable to ignore it.

So let's consider the slangy and often automatic response to praise or thanks that is rapidly saturating our current culture—"no problem." When the word *problem* is included in our reply, then if our audience is actually paying attention to us, we risk having their brains register the word *problem*. Just like your brains thought about desk chairs and cotton candy, our audience may hear *problem* and then consciously or subconsciously think about the potential for a problem. A problem is a negative, a detriment—it suggests damage and adverse outcomes. So why suggest it? Why introduce the idea of an adverse outcome? In the customer service world, many customer-facing employees are actually prohibited from using the phrase "no problem" for this exact reason. It creates a risk that customers will actually believe that they might have created a problem. It risks leaving customers with a feeling of negativity.

Additionally, many people believe that the phrase "no problem" characterizes a positive statement of praise as, instead, a burden or inconvenience that we are forgiving. So besides introducing a potential problem, we also risk having suggested that our business partners' praise was an inconvenience. While theoretically the two negatives ("no" and "problem") should have canceled each other out, in practice, that's not what happens. Instead, the two negatives simply turn what should have been a positive interaction into a negative one. Again, gratitude is expressed, but it does not appear to have been meaningfully received. These are not winning conditions.

Unfortunately, like my deflection, slang responses like "no problem" (or its pal "no worries") have become largely routine and robotic for many people. But in a nuanced and subtle way, they risk undermining the winning outcomes for which we're striving. We can all do better. The point is, don't be a christine and insinuate that the work wasn't a big deal, and don't be a joe and introduce a potential problem or inconvenience. Be an Amazing Roselyn. It's easy, and it doesn't take any extra time at all to present yourself and your work in a way that inspires positivity, not dismissal. Do this for the big things and do this for the little things. Remember:

The way that Roselyn interacted with our colleagues drove them to feel a particular way about her. She was creating her own winning conditions. You can do this, too.

In my case, once I became consciously aware of banishing my typical self-deprecating language and replacing it with something more positive, thankful, authentic, and uplifting, I began to move closer to winning conditions. I noticed a distinct shift in response to my work. I felt more valued and more significant. You can, too. Try it. The next time that your work is praised or someone expresses admiration for your efforts, thoughtfully and graciously say thank you without disqualifying yourself or your work.

Now admittedly, I don't always remember. Sometimes I fall again into unintentional blindness and go back into my mindless and automatic response, not because I am careless, and not because I am flawed, but because I am human and I possess a human brain. But the more often I can remind myself to think about the winning conditions, the more likely I am to achieve them.

This book is your wake-up call to consciously and purposefully look for the six fingers, the missing ear, the chest-pounding gorilla. Whatever the situation, you'll begin to recognize the details that matter, and you'll begin to make small changes in your behaviors to improve your outcomes. This book will help you understand which details will especially make a difference in the workplace. They will also help you outside the workplace! Whether your role is to deliver strategy, care, service, ideas, advice, lessons, products, technology, or anything else, *consciously* setting up winning conditions around the delivery of your work will maximize your impact and your success. It's easy.

You will step out of the shadows, too.

CHAPTER 2

CONSIDER
THE PAST

Have you ever been to one of those escape rooms? If not, here's how they work. Eight to ten people are "locked" in a room that usually has some theme—maybe space mission or spy shack or Egyptian tomb or murder mystery. Over the course of exactly sixty minutes, you must find clues and solve puzzles that lead to more clues and puzzles to find and solve, repeatedly, until you at last find the key or combination or instructions that will release you from the locked room. The whole experience is quite creative. Your mission might require you to order books on a bookshelf so that, when read from left to right, the titles on the spines provide the next clue. Maybe you find some foreign cash and a cell phone, and you figure out that you need to dial the serial number on the cash to hear the next clue on the phone's prerecorded voice mail message. Anyway, while you're finding the clues and solving the puzzles, a giant clock on the wall counts down from sixty minutes to zero, and the goal is to escape before your hour is up. And before you have an anxiety attack from the countdown itself.

Now, if your group is having trouble, you will receive some helpful hints via a television screen or audio system that will activate if you're stuck. But despite the hints, it's still pretty hard to escape.

Those who do escape get to pose for a team photo outside the room with congratulatory posters that say things like "Winner!" and "We did it!" and "Mission Complete!" Those who don't escape still get signs and a photo, but you're stuck with "Crashed & Burned" and "Epic Fail" and "Help!" Ah, it's all in good fun. I did an escape room with a group of pals from MIT, and we did NOT escape in time. Nonetheless, we had an absolute blast.

What's interesting about an escape room is that when you are first locked in, it looks like you're in an ordinary room. It's decorated to your theme, yes, but otherwise simply stocked and sparsely decorated. You might see one puzzle to be solved that's right there in front of you. But to escape this room, you need to understand more than that one puzzle. The escape requires finding many clues and solving many puzzles. So you look around this room, and you begin to find and solve. Fifteen minutes, thirty minutes, forty-five minutes in, you're still finding clues and solving puzzles that you originally had no idea were there. But each new thing that you find and solve brings you one step closer to the solution, the win, the escape. You see, to escape this room, all of the details are necessary, not just the one that was staring you in the face the moment you walked in the room.

It's that way in the workplace, too. Finding your win usually involves more than this one project or one meeting or one problem that's staring you in the face today. There are almost always other details present, perhaps hidden. But if you can find them and use them in your solution, then you have a much better chance of achieving that positive outcome you seek.

We've already learned that sometimes we live mindlessly—not because we are lazy or careless, but because we are human. We learned about conscious awareness and how making small changes in our behaviors based on our conscious observations can notably improve our outcomes. So let's apply our conscious awareness to our surroundings, taking notice of that which is visible and probing deeper for that which may not be visible. Understanding the full situation will enable us to provide even more effective work or solutions or ideas. We will better understand our business partners' responses and motivations, and we can therefore more effectively address their concerns, needs, and wants.

THE INFLUENCE OF PRIOR EVENTS

Humans are learning creatures. We repeat or modify our behavior and our decisions through experience. If we do something and receive a positive response, we'll want to do that again. It feels good to succeed, so we look to succeed again. If we do something and fail, we'll probably stop doing it that way. We'll modify our behavior and decisions and try again. We'll course correct. We'll improve. Or we may stop doing it completely. We'll find a way to succeed, or at the very least, we'll stop failing. It feels bad to fail.

This is important because whether your current project or work is accepted is not based only on your current work or project. It's based on more than what's staring you in the face today. It's also heavily influenced by the past successes and failures of your organization and business partners. How do the past events, projects, or outcomes influence the decisions and judgments that are being made about your work today? Is it possible that your work could be devalued based on factors having absolutely nothing to do with the work itself? How can we avoid this outcome?

I've seen a repeated phenomenon that often plays out with new hires—I bet you've seen this, too. Of course, new hires are by their nature plunked into the middle of workplace events and projects with initially little (if any) knowledge of what has happened in the organization previously. Perhaps the new hire wants to make a great first impression and so they quickly offer up a new idea. Maybe they want to streamline a process, improve a report, implement a new technology, or otherwise update the way that we've always done something. New Hire thinks their idea is so perfect, we must implement it immediately! New Hire cannot believe no one has ever thought of this! New Hire is going to be such a winner! You see, New Hire has done this before in their last organization and learned that it works—New Hire wants to feel this success again.

What's weird is that when New Hire suggests this brilliant new idea, nobody listens. They ignore New Hire completely, or just tell New Hire it's not a good idea. But it IS a good idea! Why won't people listen?

Well, if New Hire had stopped for a moment and dug a little deeper, taken notice of that which is visible and probed deeper for that which may not be visible, perhaps New Hire would have found that a similar idea was suggested, tested, and failed ten new hires ago. Then another similar idea was suggested, tested, and failed nine new hires ago. Then suggested, tested, and failed eight new hires ago. And seven new hires ago. Six. Five. Four . . . and just like the song "100 Bottles of Beer on the Wall," this routine gets old quickly. Even you, dear reader, are probably already ready for the end of this paragraph. You'd ignore New Hire, too. So now when they suggest their great new idea . . . well, we're not trying that again. Been there, done that. You see, this idea might have succeeded for New Hire in their last organization (hence, why New Hire wants to do it again), but it was an epic fail for us multiple times (hence, why we are now avoiding it at all cost). It's probably easier to just ignore New Hire. New Hire never even bothered to ask us how we felt about this. New Hire will end up holding the "Crashed & Burned" sign. This is NOT the sign they expected.

What could New Hire have done differently to have a greater chance of successfully implementing their idea and holding the "Winner!" sign instead?

Let's think about this a bit more globally. Let's consider any interaction that might occur in the course of doing business. We might be engaging with our internal teams, like our managers, direct reports, or other cross-functional teams, or we might be engaging with external business partners, like vendors, consultants, and customers. This might be a routine check-in or the big meeting we've been anticipating for months. Each of these engagements involves humans, who are learning creatures. If our colleagues have succeeded in the past, then they will probably look to repeat the work or project in a similar way. It feels good to succeed, and they want to succeed again. If our business partners have not succeeded in the past, then they will probably do things differently, or discontinue the work or project completely. It feels bad to fail. So you'll likely have a better outcome if you can understand what has transpired *for your colleagues and for the organization* in the moments, days, months, or sometimes years before this meeting. It will help you anticipate how they may judge your work, recommendations, or ideas. Remember:

> *Whether your current project or work is accepted is not based entirely on your current work or project. It's also heavily influenced by past successes and failures of your organization and business partners.*

Sometimes I think of this like starting a movie from the beginning instead of the middle. When you start a movie from the beginning, you understand the characters and their decisions. You can better anticipate what might happen next. The movie makes sense. But if you've ever tried to watch a movie starting in the middle, it's harder to figure out. You might expect a different outcome or be confused over details or behaviors. That's why when you start watching a movie from the middle, you may ask your friend or partner, "What did I miss?"

Ask this in the workplace, too. *What did I miss?*

▸ What ideas, processes, or formats have worked well in the past, and why were they successful? Think about if you can replicate those conditions again, create something comparable, or create something even better.

▶ What ideas, processes, or formats have not been previously successful? Why did they fail? Consider how you can correct the prior flaws and offer an improved service or solution. Consider whether the environment has changed sufficiently over time such that attempting the same thing again may provide a more successful outcome this time.

▶ What pleased your colleagues in the past? How can you please them again?

▶ What concerned or aggravated your colleagues in the past? How can you position your work to avoid additional concern?

▶ What are your colleagues specifically seeking to improve now? What problems would they like to solve? Why do these problems exist?

Think about New Hire. Ah, New Hire. They should have sought out some history. What did they miss? Instead of immediately bombarding their colleagues with their idea, they should have first tried to understand WHAT had previously been suggested, and tested, and failed. They should have considered WHY those past attempts may have failed and articulated in their pitch all the reasons that this idea or current environment is different and will lead to success THIS TIME. They should have shared their unique skills or perspective that weren't involved previously but will contribute to the success now. They should have articulated a new future based on a revised foundation.

Here is my idea. I know we've previously tried something similar and it hasn't worked out, but my idea is different and here's why. Here's why I will make this work.

Now that is a great New Hire. Seeking out what transpired in the past and building a brighter future from it boosts value and the likelihood of success. It's a detail that matters.

Let's pretend that when New Hire seeks the history, they learn that related projects within this organization had been successful. Given that information, they should identify and articulate how their idea can replicate, build on, or enhance these past successes.

Here is my idea. I know we've previously implemented a related system and it was a great success. My idea builds on these successes in this way, so we can continue to escalate our positive results.

New Hire has leveraged people's propensity to learn and improve. Plus, New Hire won't just look like a copycat—their colleagues will see that they gave this some serious thought.

Now, I could have shared that entire example but replaced "New Hire" with any role, any tenure, and any situation (in or out of the workplace). Every meeting, engagement, or interaction benefits by understanding what transpired previously. Even if you've worked in an organization for years, probing further for more details will help you understand how to best approach the current engagement.

A good friend of mine, also named Holly but not my high school bestie, manages the flow of patients through the emergency room at a children's hospital. When I say "manages," I mean that she runs the entire department. She has been with the hospital for fourteen years. She is incredibly successful and highly effective at her job, and she always begins her improvements with some research. She doesn't immediately draw conclusions or decide how it must necessarily be, based on her current view. Instead, she tries to understand everything she can about the full situation surrounding the problem she's addressing. Why is this the process? Why was it originally set up this way? Why hasn't it been changed previously? What parts have been updated? Have any attempted updates been unsuccessful?

Why? She considers the people involved—both current and past. She remembers that many other engagements led up to this moment. There is a history, and it is important. And because she looks for the full story, she can better develop and articulate her planned solution, leading to an increased likelihood of success. Holly is usually left holding the "Mission Complete!" sign.

Maybe you'd like to ask your manager for a raise or a promotion. After all, you've already spent a reasonable time at your current salary or level. Find some history that can help you articulate your pitch. See if you can find out the general types of experience or years of service of others who have previously been promoted to the level you'd like to achieve. If you're unable to find out this information by probing specifically within your company, an internet search might help illuminate the answers for similar types of roles in your industry. What skills did the successful candidates have? What similar or additional skills do you have that are unique and beneficial? In most cases, going into a meeting without any information about prior events is not going to benefit your conversation. A little research goes a long way—and if you can include some concrete information in your pitch, you just might have a better chance of getting it.

Whatever the topic, audience, project, or proposal, find out more about the past events. The History Checklist on the following page can help you formulate a discovery plan—consider it for all departments, functions, and customers that are affected by your work. You may have additional questions depending on your particular situation. Ask your teammates. Ask your manager. Ask your direct reports. Ask people on another team or in another department. Just ask. Probing deeper will enhance and guide your approach and allow you to provide even more effective solutions. You'll better understand and anticipate responses and motivations.

But there's another major benefit of asking for more. I learned this through an experience outside the workplace—as a parent—when I was the one being questioned.

HISTORY CHECKLIST

❏ Has this idea, work, or project been attempted before?

❏ Did it succeed?

❏ Why or why not?

❏ What parts of the past work were particularly valuable?

❏ What parts of the past work were detrimental?

❏ What areas were liked/disliked?

❏ Who was a champion of the past work?

❏ Did anyone potentially undermine past work? Why?

❏ How did our technical, legal, contractual, or other regulatory limitations affect the outcome or idea?

❏ What was the time frame?

❏ Do you think the time frame was too aggressive or too lengthy?

❏ What was the cost?

❏ Was this cost viewed as too much, too little, or about right?

❏ Has the environment changed since this idea was previously attempted?

❏ How might this new environment affect the outcome of your current proposal differently than the previous attempt?

FEELING HEARD

Years ago, when my children were small, our family was enjoying a fun day at the beach. My daughter, Elise, was about eleven months old, and in one split second she beelined straight to the water. I quickly jumped up and grabbed her arm before she crawled into the ocean, and in the process, her elbow dislocated. This was no longer a fun day at the beach. Needless to say, I felt like a horrible mother, and I immediately brought her to the emergency room. Apparently this situation is not entirely uncommon. There is even a colloquial name for the condition—nursemaid's elbow. It comes from the idea that a nursemaid (an old-fashioned name for a nanny or babysitter) would pick a child up by the hand, and the undeveloped bones of the elbow in the small child could quite easily pop out. Anyway, the doctor popped her elbow back into place, and we went on our way.

About five days later, my family was at my dad's house celebrating his birthday. It was a wonderful party, until my little Elise fell under the kitchen table and split open her eyebrow on the table leg. She clearly needed stitches, but my husband, Keith, and I were anxious about bringing her to the same ER again. What if Child Protective Services claimed we were unfit parents? Of course, we brought her in anyway. The health-care providers asked Keith and me many questions in many different ways about this second accident, and also the first. They questioned us separately and together. They repeated the same questions, but sometimes with a new one tossed in. They left no stone unturned. Once the nurses, doctors, and other health-care professionals felt that they fully understood the situation, the surgeon stitched up her eyebrow and sent us home, confident that we were, in fact, good parents. The ER team went beyond the superficial appearance of two medical emergencies just days apart, and instead leveraged her history—her documented medical records and our repeated and separate explanations of what had occurred—to understand the correct future course of action. (Side note: I'm happy to report that Elise hasn't had any out-of-the-ordinary medical needs in the sixteen years since this awful week.)

Nevertheless, here's what I learned from this experience. I learned that it feels good to be able to share your side of things. It feels good when someone asks you your opinion and shows interest in your perspective. It feels good when you know the solution takes your knowledge into account. It feels good to know that past problems can be corrected and successes can be enhanced based on your input. When someone takes a moment to ask about the past, it feels good. Even with a trip to the ER, I was greatly comforted by the fact that the health-care providers allowed us ample opportunity to share the backstory. I felt heard. The situation was optimized, and we all left satisfied. Those are winning conditions.

So let's draw on this example. Have you ever found yourself in a situation where you felt it was necessary to explain your side of things in order to direct the best outcome? Have you ever worried that someone might make an incorrect judgment unless you're able to share this backstory? Have you ever acted or made a decision based on pure logic, but your actions were later questioned as surprising or illogical by others who didn't know the background? When you are provided an opportunity to share your knowledge and perspective, don't you feel notably more positive about the situation and more confident in the outcome?

We can see that seeking the past is more than learning and articulating how and why our work can be more successful. It turns out that the mere act of *asking* for that history causes our colleagues to actually *feel better*. People will feel more positively about us and our work simply because we asked for their perspective. People want to be heard. People want to be understood. Helping teammates and colleagues and clients and customers share their side of the story is winning conditions.

The simple act of asking your colleagues their history, their side of the story, or their perspective causes them to feel more positively about you and your work.

Let's put it all together. You want to look beyond the work or the project that's right in front of you. Take notice of that which is visible, and probe deeper for that which may not be visible. Remember that whether your current project or work is accepted is not based only on your current work or project. It's also heavily influenced by the past successes and failures of your organization and business partners. When you understand the full situation, you can provide an even more effective solution, because you can:

▸ Anticipate your colleagues' responses, motivations, fears, and desires,

▸ Develop work or solutions that will build off past success or pivot to a new approach for past fails—both of which are winning conditions,

▸ Articulate a bright future based on a new, improved foundation, and

▸ Help others feel happier and more satisfied with you, your work, and your approach.

Just ask: *What did I miss?*

Everyone involved benefits. So, now you are becoming consciously aware. You are finding the clues that will better enable you to achieve the win, the solution, the success. Hold that "Winners!" sign high above your head! In the next chapter, we'll continue to build on these ideas about becoming consciously aware of the bigger picture. In fact, beyond a history that you might not have seen on first glance, there could also be additional people exerting influence over your outcomes—people who may not even be present at your meetings or appear to have decisioning authority for your projects.

Meet me in Chapter 3!

My daughter Elise (far right) and her friends celebrating their escape from an escape room.

BUILD A COALITION OF SUPPORT

In the spring of 2017, I set out to fulfill a sixteen-year dream of competing on CBS's hit reality television show *Survivor*. In this thirty-nine-day game, sixteen to twenty strangers are marooned in some undeveloped area of the world. Past locations have included remote beaches on islands like Borneo, Fiji, and the Philippines, and remote mainland areas such as Kenya, Brazil, and China. Players live outside for the duration of the game in whatever makeshift shelter they can build, using whatever natural supplies they can find. There is little food, perhaps a handful of cooked rice to eat a day, plus whatever meat you're lucky enough to catch, like the occasional fish or the occasional rat. There is no clean water in which to wash. There is no soap, shampoo, razors, deodorant, mirrors, hairbrushes, toilets, or toilet paper. There is no technology or electricity. There is no privacy. There is no contact with the outside world.

But despite its name, *Survivor* is not actually a survival game. It is an extreme strategy game. Players live together in teams, called tribes, and vote each other out of the game one by one over thirty-nine days until there is just one sole survivor who has outwitted, outplayed, and outlasted all the rest. This sole survivor wins one million dollars. One million dollars!

The entire adventure is filmed twenty-four hours a day for all thirty-nine days and later broadcast on primetime television. When my season of *Survivor* (Season 35—*Survivor: Heroes vs. Healers vs. Hustlers*) began to air on TV in the fall of 2017, the most common question I was asked about the so-called greatest social experiment on television was, "Is it real?"

Yes, Virginia, it is real. We really live outside on the beach. We really are starving. We really are dirty. We really are playing. I really did not wash my hair or brush my teeth for thirty-nine days (yep, almost six weeks). People really lose vast amounts of weight because there is practically nothing to eat. The rats really chew holes in our clothes at night. Our conversations are self-started and our actions are self-motivated. There are no retakes. There are no lines to memorize. There are no scripts, no cues, no predeveloped stories. *Survivor* is truly reality TV.

So then, if this game is so real, is there more to be found if we probe deeper? Is there more to the game than what you see on your television screens? Yes and yes. Always look deeper.

Let's take a peek behind the scenes. That one-on-one conversation that you saw play out from the comfort of your family room sofa was never one on one. If you probe deeper, you'll see a full camera and sound crew in view, with a large array of heavy technical equipment. You'll see a comprehensive medical staff evaluating players repeatedly throughout the game to ensure the utmost safety and health care. You'll see captains transporting players by boat to the challenges that begin on docks in the middle of the ocean, because the players surely didn't swim all the way out there. You'll see divers underwater during difficult ocean challenges to ensure players don't drown—and to film the underwater footage. You'll see work crews who've built those incredible challenge courses, standing ready to fix any parts that may be damaged by weather before the players even have a chance to compete. You will see far more than the sixteen to twenty castaways that have come to play, plus our beloved host. In fact, if you probe deeper, you will see more than six hundred crew members[3] who are diligently working behind the scenes to create the views that you and millions of others enjoy from your family room sofas every Wednesday night. And here's the important part—the success of the show would not be possible without this behind-the-scenes, originally unseen support crew.

It's that way in the workplace, too. We need a support crew—even if you don't see them at first. The bigger your support crew, the more likely you are to succeed. That's because it's easier to achieve a positive result when other people are supporting your work. It's more likely you'll be celebrated and recognized when other people are supporting your work. The more people that support your work, the more likely you are to come out with a win.

We learned in the last chapter that we can't automatically assume we know the whole story based on what we see at first glance. We learned that probing for the past history allows us to optimize and articulate our valuable work. It allows our business partners to feel satisfied and heard. Let's push this idea a bit further.

Winning conditions is also looking beyond our immediate managers, teams, or customers to build support from anyone else who may be impacted by our work. It's understanding how our work impacts others at different levels and in different roles—and respecting and honoring these others. It's recognizing what would compel them to support our work and support our projects. It's leveraging that army of support to optimize our likelihood of success.

I once was briefly brought into a consulting project in which a data science team was building a new "data lake," which is really just a neat name for a way to store data. There were some unexpected challenges throughout the process, so the project was taking a lot longer than expected. Because of the delays, the team was concerned that their manager might soon just cancel the whole thing. When I first met with the team, I asked them some questions, like:

---

3   Ross, Dalton. "All Hands on Deck: Behind the Scenes of a Survivor Marooning." *Entertainment Weekly*, February 20, 2019. https://ew.com/tv/2019/02/20/survivor-edge-of-extinction-marooning/

PART 1: EMBRACE THE BIGGER PICTURE

Who will be using the data lake?
Why do they need the data lake?
How do the users feel about the data lake?

Their answers left my jaw on the ground. But not really, because I actually see this too often.

Teams A, B, and C will use the data lake.
The data lake will enable faster and easier use, capture, and storage of information.
They don't know about it. We thought we'd build it first and then tell them.

Well, of course this great project was at risk! If no one else knew it was coming, how could they support it? You see, it's important to think beyond pleasing your manager (or whoever is the gatekeeper of your great work). If you can find a way to build support with the many other people in or out of your organization who might benefit from it, then your manager will see:

Wow, look at all this support.
Wow, you really are great.
Wow, your work and work style are positively impacting so many others.
Wow, your work is making a positive difference.
Wow, you are a winner.

In this case, even though the project was behind schedule, support from Teams A, B, and C to build and deliver the data lake would provide a greater likelihood that the project could be championed to completion. But Teams A, B, and C would need to know about it to support it. They'd need to know that the data lake would enable faster and easier use, capture, and storage of information. They'd need to know how their own work would greatly benefit from this data lake.

Beyond recognizing what would encourage others to support our work, winning conditions also involves understanding what might cause others to resist or undermine our work. We want to recognize when we are unfavorably affecting others in different levels, roles, or functions and consider if there might be a better way that doesn't leave a trail of negativity or harm.

Consider the data lake. Truthfully, if I were on Team A, B, or C, and you came to me *after* this thing was already built, then I might be a little irritated that you never bothered to ask me if I even needed a data lake. I might feel somewhat bulldozed into a new storage system that makes perfect sense to you but might be incredibly confusing to me. By keeping me in the dark, I might think that you didn't respect me or respect my work or my decisions.

Ultimately, understanding what might cause others to support or resist our work are details that matter. So let's explore how we can build coalitions of support.

THINKING BEYOND A WELL-FOCUSED STRATEGY

When most of us think about creating a high-quality work product or positive outcome, we tend to think strategically. Thinking strategically means that we thoughtfully create goals with rational, measured care. We methodically design the appropriate tasks required to carry out some particular outcome or advantage. We meticulously and purposefully analyze problems and opportunities. We carefully consider our work with an eye to maximum efficiency and effectiveness. A well-focused, strategic mindset is the backbone of our excellent work. Essentially, we think about what we need to accomplish, and we accomplish it. We build that data lake to enable faster and easier use, capture, and storage of information. Simple.

But we need to be careful that we don't focus so intently on the strategy that we become unintentionally blind to all else. You see, a directed focus from only the strategic point of view ignores a critical aspect of achieving success—most directed strategies will only succeed if other people support them. Basically, it's not only my manager who decides if my data lake is a success—I also need Teams A, B, and C to think it's great, because they will be the downstream users of my work.

Here's another example. A close friend of mine is a spiritual woman. Her church is a large one—probably a thousand weekly in attendance and twice that in membership. The church's mission statement is simple but clear: "Follow God's call to a new life." And the church members went ahead and did just that. Members joyfully created multiple ministries with many different aspirations, tasks, and goals. There were support groups, men's groups, women's groups, and children's groups meeting on various schedules and with varying objectives. There surely was something to satisfy many different levels of spirituality and availability—but the wide window of options afforded by a simple mission statement ultimately led to a giant hodgepodge of worship groups with little consistency or regularity to the programming.

So the pastor decided to tighten up the strategic direction of the church. His goal was to focus the programming to achieve better uniformity and stability within the church's offerings. After carefully analyzing the current miscellany of schedules and considering the potential opportunities, he implemented a new strategic plan that moved all of the short-term Bible study groups onto a long-term, uniform schedule. This thoughtfully developed plan allowed for the most efficient and effective programming across the longer horizon. Simple.

The pastor didn't anticipate that the improvement in scheduling would cause a deterioration in membership. In fact, program participation in all areas declined. Why did this happen? Let's take a step back for a moment to examine some underlying forces that were influencing this situation.

Decades ago, organizational theorists Michael Tushman and David Nadler suggested that optimal workplace performance occurs when ideal dynamics exist between certain organizational elements, like strategy, culture, and power. The areas Tushman and Nadler identified—strategy, culture, and power—are also useful for understanding how we can most effectively develop our support crews and avoid an unexpected or sudden deterioration of that support.

At its most straightforward and basic level, other people naturally tend to support or resist strategic initiatives (strategy) based on how these initiatives will affect their own *current positioning*. Current positioning includes:

1. how people typically do their work (culture); and

2. how much control people believe they have over their own work and decisions, and within the organization (power).

So when you think about building a coalition of support, you need to think about how your thoughtfully and meticulously developed work will impact others' current positioning. In this case, despite the pastor's carefully planned strategy, members of the church felt negatively impacted. They preferred short-term commitments. The shorter modules had been a great way to train and develop future leaders, but the longer commitments didn't allow members to practice leadership skills on different people in different groups. Ministry leaders were upset that they had lost the ability to make decisions. The women's ministry in particular was hard hit. The shorter modules had aligned beautifully with the school calendar and holidays, but the longer modules didn't accommodate the moms' family responsibilities.

Let's explore the two main components of positioning so that we can better understand how the impact of our work on other people will affect our ability to build a coalition of support. As you read through this chapter, think about the people, teams, departments, or groups that are impacted by your work in any way.

WORK HABITS AND COMPANY CULTURE

Work behaviors and habits are sometimes referred to as "company culture." Note, in this context we are not talking about culture as relates to particular nations, races, ethnicities, religions, or family customs. Instead, we're reflecting on the culture of the *organization itself*, or how people do their work and describe their work environment. Just like ethnic cultures, work cultures are a way of life. They are the ingrained ways that we generally behave at work or within our organizations, including our daily habits.

For example, maybe in your office, team meetings happen every Monday or every day or not at all. Maybe you have flex time, or maybe everybody punches the clock at exactly 9 a.m. and 5 p.m. Maybe your office has run the same programs for the past fifty years—sure, another way might be faster, but you like it this way. Maybe you always align your ministries with the school calendar and holidays. These are all examples of organizational culture: the norms that are habitual, ingrained, and expected.

For many people, consistency in work habits is a comforting routine. It gives people a break from constant decision making, staves off the potential fear of the unknown, and diminishes the need to direct brain cells to an activity that perhaps can be completed on autopilot. Consistency creates order in a world that can sometimes feel chaotic. That's why for some, change—or the lack of consistency—can be scary, or difficult, or cumbersome, or labor intensive. Sometimes change can be just plain annoying. So it's important to consciously consider how your work is going to affect the current culture. If your work aligns with the typical habits that others enjoy, or offers more favorable norms, then this is a massive benefit. Celebrate this alignment to build your coalition of supporters. Clearly articulate the alignment to further boost your value proposition. *"My initiative supports our existing culture and processes, so it will be easy to understand and adopt."*

Make sure that when you are analyzing impact, you consider the impact from the *others'* point of view—not your own. You can't just automatically assume that everyone else will like your work simply because you like your own work. Will Teams A, B, and C think that your data lake is an improvement to their current processes? Will Teams A, B, and C think your data lake is easy to implement, learn, and understand? Does the data lake offer more favorable norms from the point of view of Teams A, B, and C? If you believe that yes, the new processes will definitely be more favorable, then start talking with Teams A, B, and C about this early in the process. Get them excited about the potential! Build your coalition of support.

What if you find that your work might negatively impact current culture or current habits? This is what happened in the church. The members preferred short-term commitments, practicing leadership skills with varied groups, and folding in schedules around the school calendar. They felt that the long-term programming negatively impacted their preferred norms.

In these cases, consider if alternative solutions exist that are similarly effective but less disruptive. For example, perhaps the pastor can streamline the programming for all groups except the women's ministry, which faces distinct and specific conflicts from the school calendar. Maybe they can provide additional time for all groups to convert to the new programming, so that the members have time to comfortably adopt new norms. Perhaps there is a new way to train future ministry leaders within the long-term programming that still allows for practicing new skills on varied groups. Clearly articulating your thoughtful consideration of the potential impacts and possible alternatives will boost your value proposition. *"My initiative may disrupt aspects of our existing culture, so I have implemented the following solutions to minimize those disruptions."*

Another way to build support is to include some affected members in the brainstorming of solutions. Not only can they potentially generate useful options, but allowing others input means they are less likely to feel bulldozed into compliance. Instead, the included members would become early advocates for success of the new strategies. *"My initiative may disrupt aspects of our existing culture, but I have worked together with members of your team to find solutions to minimize the disruptions."*

Lastly, if disruption to current norms is unavoidable—and sometimes disruption *is* necessary for the health of the organization—then empathetically and honestly discuss the situation with those affected. Share potential downstream positive impacts. Be respectful. Despite a deterioration in positioning, you may be able to create support through honest communication and respect. *"My initiative will unavoidably disrupt aspects of our existing culture, and I know that can be challenging. I'm sorry about that. We are implementing this initiative in order to gain in these ways [X, Y, and Z] and I hope that makes sense, even though this is difficult. I very much respect you and your great work, and I'm sorry that you may need to bear a burden of this."* While no words may be completely ideal, something empathetic and respectful is probably better than radio silence.

Remember:

> *To some people, change can be scary, difficult, or just plain annoying. Therefore, it's important to consciously consider how your work is going to affect the current culture of the organization. By celebrating alignment or improvement, and managing potential negative disruption, you can work to respectfully and thoughtfully create a coalition of support.*

Let's suppose that work hours in your organization are a traditional 9 a.m. to 5 p.m., but you'd like to move to flex time. Specifically, you'd like to work 7 a.m. to 3 p.m., so that you can accommodate some personal responsibilities. Winning conditions means that when you pitch your case, you go beyond articulating how you'll get your own work done under the new arrangement. You'll also need to address how your new schedule will impact the typical work habits of others. Are you expecting that team meetings previously scheduled between 3 p.m. and 5 p.m. will now need to be held earlier in the day? Can you think of some reasons that this culture change may benefit others on the team? For example, perhaps holding all meetings before 3 p.m. will allow all employees uninterrupted focus in the afternoon. Would this new scheduling harm anyone else on the team? Can you solve for that disruption? Might others also want to engage in flex time? Is there a way that this change can benefit the entire organization? Are there potential unintended downstream impacts? Consideration and articulation of these cultural impacts will enable you to more likely be awarded that flex time.

My mother, also named Christine, built and ran a small medical education company. During the company's twenty-year run, the employees developed close working and personal relationships and a strong company culture. For example, everyone (yes, everyone—from the president to the summer intern) ate lunch together in a big conference room from noon to 1 p.m. Every day. Lunch at noon. In the conference room. During this time, stories were shared, problems were solved, relationships were strengthened. It was a joyful, consistent, stress-free break in the day. This was their culture, and it reinforced the strong and positive working environment within the company.

As she approached retirement, my mom decided to sell her company. The employees remained at the same physical location, but now they reported up through a large pharmaceutical advertising agency. This agency instituted a more flexible arrangement that encouraged employees to stagger their one-hour lunches anytime from 11 a.m. to 2 p.m. This strategy was designed to eliminate full workforce breaks in the workday and offer additional flexibility to the employees. Simple. The employees complied, and their lunches were staggered. In the small office people now went different ways at different times.

But the strategy that was meant for accommodation and continuity of work clashed with the intrinsic culture of the smaller organization. Work began to suffer. While previously client work could be dependably completed before noon and after 1 p.m., now there was no consistency to attendance. Workers couldn't always find their colleagues when they needed them. Midday meeting scheduling became more difficult. In this case, the widening of the lunch hour actually added stress. It weakened relationships. The change in the ingrained habits was viewed as highly unfavorable.

Ultimately the employees reverted back to their prior norms. They all chose to once again eat lunch together from noon to 1 p.m. in the conference room. They wanted their culture back. They viewed the new strategy as a deterioration in their own positions, and so they opposed it.

Can you think of an example within your workplace when a thoughtful strategic decision was in opposition to your established culture? How did employees react? Do you think this could have been handled better?

The next time you deliver your work, consciously consider its impact on others. Clearly articulate how your work, idea, or solution aligns with or improves the existing culture. If there's a potential negative disruption, then offer proactive solutions for thoughtfully mitigating the impact. Include some impacted members in your decision making. They may generate additional solutions and are less likely to feel bulldozed into compliance. Create support through empathetic, honest, and respectful communication.

Let's now consider the second aspect of positioning, which involves your work's impact on the amount of control other people have over work, decisions, and outcomes.

POWER AND CONTROL

Let's face it: many people in the workplace are self-focused, and for good reason—thoughtfully directing our own work in a positive way provides us personal and financial success and satisfaction. It's human nature to want to maintain control of our own decisions and directions. Therefore, most people don't see things from the angle of "What is the most rational and effective strategy for the organization?" Instead, the more common perspective is, "What's in it for me? How does that initiative affect me and affect the control and authority I have over my work and my team? How does it affect my level of influence and power within the organization? How does it affect my ability to drive my own positive outcomes?"

People will naturally seek to maintain control of their own decisions and directed focus. Winning conditions is recognizing and articulating the value and impact of your work from the perspective of "What's in it for them?"

People generally view an increase of their own responsibility, influence, or authority as a positive. Therefore, if your work allows others to maintain or increase control, or improves their success or satisfaction, then they will likely support it and support you. In this case, you should articulate how the future state is preferable to the current state. *"Here's how you and your team will benefit from this solution."* You will build a coalition of advocates.

Conversely, people generally will view an erosion of their own responsibility, influence, or authority as a negative. Therefore, if your work takes control away from others, or they perceive a deterioration in their own ability to drive personal success or satisfaction, then you'll need to thoughtfully manage the disruption. Can you find another solution that allows for continuity of authority? If not, then can you think about how to empathetically and honestly communicate the change? *"Here's how you and your team will be impacted by this. Let's work together to figure this out."* Try not to bulldoze affected people into compliance, but instead include them in the solutioning. Treat people with dignity and respect. Even if others are made worse off by the change, it may be possible to turn a potential adversary into an advocate through honesty and integrity.

Remember the church? "Ministry leaders were upset that they had lost the ability to make decisions that were right for their members." The new strategy resulted in a loss of decision-making power for the ministry leaders. This was a big deal to the leaders. Perhaps including the ministry leaders in the development of the scheduling strategy, or finding a way to allow them to maintain some control within their ministries, would help build support for the long-term programming.

My good friend Suzanne is a leader in the retail space. She found herself managing a difficult power struggle when she was put in charge of the largest project her division had ever executed. There was a lot at stake, including profit, existing and new business, and the reputation of the organization, division, leaders, and products. Because there was so much attention on the initiative, not one, but five (!) executives insisted on being the executive sponsor. Each of the five wanted the ultimate control. Why? They each wanted to be able to claim they had personally made it happen. Each wanted the power. Each wanted the utmost influence and authority.

Suzanne was known within her industry and organization as an excellent relationship builder. She had a great deal of experience and had led dozens of complex projects before. But nothing had prepared her for the conflicts that occurred during those executive sponsor meetings. Each of the five executives had a completely different set of demands. They disagreed on practically everything. The constant conflict and competing interests pushed the project timeline further and further behind. As each demanded more power, each of the others sensed a loss of power. This seemed to be a no-win situation.

The solution? Suzanne took a hard look at the situation from the point of view of "What's in it for them?" She approached the sponsors and laid out their individual futures if the group continued down this path. Namely, continuing in this manner would result in a failed outcome and damaged reputations. She clearly articulated what would be in it for them if they made some changes. She proposed that two of the five act as coexecutive sponsors and the other three become the executive steering committee. She proposed controls and decisions that would be the responsibility of each. She provided each with a level of control and oversight that allowed them a sense of responsibility without such blatant overlap.

This was negotiation, diplomacy, alliance building, and conflict resolution at its finest. Once the new structure was discussed, agreed upon, and put in place, the project moved quickly back on track. It concluded on time, on budget, and with outstanding financial results. Suzanne's conscious awareness of the issues, and her respectful consideration and diplomatic handling of both the strategic *and control* implications saved that entire project.

As you reflect on your work's impact on other people's perceived level of influence, authority, and power, here are some common considerations for you to think about:

▸ If your work will require approvals, make sure you go as far up the line and across, as necessary, to ensure that others don't put up roadblocks later on simply because they weren't consulted. Sometimes people view "lack of consult" as "taking away my power." A simple check-in and common courtesy go a long way.

▸ If your work touches other departments or groups, make sure to inform these other departments or groups up front about your work, so it's not perceived that you are planning to diabolically impose on their "turf." Again, a simple check-in and common courtesy go a long way. Tell Teams A, B, and C about the data lake.

▸ Don't underestimate the strong feelings that people have about their perceived control. We learned in the last chapter that people will *feel* more positive about us and our work simply because we asked for their perspective. Similarly, they will *feel* more positive about us and our work simply because we considered and articulated thoughtfulness about their positioning. Often, people don't like to feel bulldozed into accepting something over which they had absolutely no control, input, or influence.

A friend shared with me a story about her local community's struggling middle school, which recently hired a new principal. Upon joining the administration, the new principal quickly noted several significant changes that she wanted to make. Recognizing that the current staff, parent-teacher association, parents, and volunteers all felt a strong sense of duty, responsibility, loyalty, and accountability to the school, the principal didn't make these changes all at once. She appropriately realized that changing too much too fast could feel like a reduction in power to the other staff and community members, and she didn't want to set up unnecessary conflict.

The principal took some time to recognize "What's in it for them?" and then responded accordingly. Staff, syllabi, and scheduling changes were implemented only after alliances were built, and the benefits and drawbacks of potential changes were thoughtfully discussed with stakeholders. She asked for feedback and listened to the various opinions and options before collaboratively deciding on a final course of action. This diplomatic consideration of the perceived power distribution ultimately allowed the principal to complete more rather than less. The brief pause allowed for greater speed and impact later. The stakeholder group of teachers, community members, parents, and volunteers felt heard and respected and, in turn, strongly supported the changes that were ultimately made. They supported the principal fully.

Sadly, the story doesn't end there. This highly effective and highly supported principal needed to take an extended leave for personal reasons. A replacement took over and immediately embarked on implementing extensive additional changes to the staffing, curriculum, and scheduling. There was no pause to consider "What's in it for them?" It was bulldozing at its best. Much conflict and aggravation ensued, with poor results, little support, and lots of undermining. The community was left dissatisfied and unhappy. The replacement principal had inadvertently eroded his own influence. These are not winning conditions.

In any organization, it's not uncommon for a new leader to make updates to staff, processes, or policies, even if the organization isn't necessarily struggling. Sometimes leaders feel the need to change things that are actually working smoothly, simply so they can feel as if they've put their fingerprints on their new role. Can you think of an example within your workplace when a strategic decision was made—either to solve a real problem, or to place fingerprints "just because"—that took power away from a person or team? How did that person or team feel about this new strategy? How was the situation handled?

The next time you deliver your work, consciously consider its impact on others' perceived levels of control. Share how others will benefit from your work or offer solutions for how you will thoughtfully handle the power shift.

You've now laid a strong foundation of success. You've learned to explore the positions of others at any level, in any role or function, who may be impacted by your work. You now consider your work's impact on typical behaviors and expected norms, and its impact on others' perceived levels of control. You thoughtfully articulate your value and the value your work brings to others. You respect others' positions, and you treat others with honesty, integrity, empathy, and respect. You create a coalition of advocates who will push for your projects to succeed. The result? Your manager or team will see:

Wow, look at all this support.
Wow, you really are great.
Wow, your work and work style are positively impacting so many others.
Wow, your work is making a positive difference.
Wow, you are a winner.

As we move forward into Chapter 4, we'll continue to explore the perspectives of others, but we'll focus on those immediately in the room, with whom you are actively working.

PART 2:

OPTIMIZE
YOUR CURRENT
ENGAGEMENTS

ACCOMMODATE DIFFERENT PERSPECTIVES

Ever since I was in the seventh grade, I've had a subscription to *GAMES* magazine. So far in my life, I've thoroughly enjoyed over four hundred monthly issues. My husband is a saint and has learned to accept that at least twenty issues are on my nightstand at all times, to satisfy any mood of puzzling on any given evening. *GAMES* magazine is filled with every puzzle you can imagine— crossword puzzles, word searches, Sudokus, cryptograms, Battleships, logic puzzles, riddles, and more.

Decades ago, *GAMES* had a feature called Eyeball Benders. In this game, close-up photos of common objects were provided, and the reader would guess the object from this unlikely view. Some photos were easier to guess, and some were nearly impossible. Some views were so obscure that it took a last-resort trip to the answer key to figure it out. But alas, even though the point of view was obscure, it was still an accurate view. Just different, is all. It's a little bit like when we took a step back from the reality TV game and saw the support crew in view. It's a new perspective, a way to look at things a little bit differently. Sometimes looking at things from a different point of view allows us to understand them better.

It's not hard to understand why different people—both in and out of the workplace—have different points of view. Varied backgrounds, interests, personalities, experiences, training, education, geographies, and other factors all contribute to our diverse attitudes, positions, or perspectives. What one person sees as the most perfect relaxing day, someone else might think is completely boring. An activity that one person considers thrilling might be viewed as recklessly dangerous by someone else. Goldilocks thought that Papa Bear's porridge was too hot; she thought Mama Bear's porridge was too cold. In each of these cases, no one is necessarily right or wrong—they simply have different points of view.

Now that we've probed deeper to find some history and developed a support crew of advocates, we'll turn to understanding the attitudes and preferences of those in the room. Winning conditions is recognizing that your colleagues have different positions and perspectives from each other—and from you. Sharing the right information about your work, in a way that will provide the greatest motivation to your business partners, will allow you to maximize their ease of understanding. It will respect and honor other opinions and views. It will allow you to showcase your work in a way that is most valued and appreciated by those who will rely on it.

So let's explore some ideas of what to share and how to share it, so you can optimize your outcomes.

WHAT TO SHARE

Aristotle once wrote, "The guest will judge better of a feast than the cook."[4] You are the cook—what do you think you should serve in your feast so that your guest is most likely to devour it? What is it that your colleague most needs to hear to best understand and appreciate your work? What will best motivate them to accept

---

4 Aristotle. *Politics*. 350 B.C.E. Translated by Benjamin Jowett, *The Complete Works of Aristotle*. Princeton: Princeton University Press, 1984.

your solutions? Here are some of the more common perspectives we might see in the workplace. This is not an exhaustive list, but instead, the ones that I have come across most frequently in my own career. There may be others that better apply in your own personal situation.

Anecdotal evidence—results of your great work are best supported through the use of anecdotes, which are short, interesting stories about a real person or event. If you tell me it's "the best," then I want to hear real stories of actual users of your work who had a positive outcome with your product or service. I am moved by the story itself, so include details so that I can actually picture this story in my mind.

Because recency bias can drive value, try and keep the stories as recent as possible. Recency bias is the human tendency to place more weight on events that happened more recently versus events that happened further in the past.

If you're presenting your work to someone who you suspect is mostly influenced by anecdotal evidence, then provide recent and compelling anecdotes to support your work.

Data—results of your great work are best supported through the use of data and evidence-based facts. If you tell me it's "the best," I want to know what data proves this. (As an actuary, this is absolutely what most moves me.) Give me statistics to reinforce the value of your work. How many people will benefit if we implement your work or idea? By what percentage will results or scores or outcomes improve? How has growth exceeded expectations? By what percentage are we seeing improvement?

If you're presenting your work or solution to someone who you suspect is mostly influenced by data, then provide various statistics to support your work.

Dollars—a nuanced version of data motivation, results of your great work are best supported through sharing information on financial gains or benefits. In the 1996 movie *Jerry Maguire*, we were introduced to the now famous movie quote "Show me the money!" In a memorable scene, football player Rod Tidwell (played by Cuba Gooding Jr.) is trying to encourage sports agent Jerry Maguire (played by Tom Cruise) to better understand him. Tidwell is clearly motivated by money—but Maguire doesn't see this. Tidwell is screaming, "Show me the money! Show me the money!" The most influential communication here happens when Jerry Maguire finally sees this deal from his customer's point of view.

With financially driven business partners, show them the money. How much will this cost to implement? How much will we earn or save? What is the impact to top- or bottom-line revenues? What is the impact to operating expenses or payroll? How is this solution better than a different solution from a financial perspective?

If you're presenting your work or solution to someone who you suspect is mostly influenced by financial impact, then provide the monetary considerations to support your work.

Expert authority—results of your great work are best supported through evidence that it is backed by experts. If you tell me it's "the best," then I want to hear about how Expert A is already using your product or idea and Expert B is recommending your product or idea. I'm inspired by learning what the experts think about your work.

If you're presenting your work or solution to someone who you suspect is mostly influenced by expert authority, then provide evidence that a real expert in this field supports your work.

Intuition/emotion—results of your great work are best supported by appealing to one's feelings. If you tell me it's "the best," then I want you to make me feel good about myself for choosing to use your product or service, or make me feel afraid, anxious, or worried if I don't use your product or service. This is a common perspective in marketing applications.

If you're presenting your work or solution to someone who you suspect is mostly influenced by intuition or emotion, then try to evoke an emotional response when you present your work.

Leader support—results of your great work are best supported through examples of how your work is supported by my leader or manager. If you tell me it's "the best," then I want to hear about how my leader believes it's the best, or how you presume my leader believes it's the best. I will align with my leader's point of view, whether expressed or assumed.

Sometimes this concept is referred to as "sunflower management," because much like a sunflower turns toward the sun regardless of its location in the sky, I will turn my attention and my support to the same products and services that my leader supports. Tell me what my leader wants—I want that, too.

If you're presenting your work or solution to someone who you suspect operates by sunflower management, then provide evidence that their leader or manager supports your work.

Outcomes—results of your great work are best supported by explaining the downstream implications of this work. If you tell me it's "the best," then I want to hear how I, my team, or my business will benefit in the long term because of your great work. I want to hear how I, my team, or my business will suffer if I don't accept your great work.

If you're presenting your work or solution to someone who you suspect is mostly influenced by outcomes, then provide potential downstream implications of use/lack of use.

Social proof—results of your great work are best supported through evidence that *other people* value your work. If you tell me it's "the best," then I want to hear why and how everyone else wants your product or wants to work with you. Tell me how my colleagues already believe in you and your product or service. Show me express or implied positive assertions from other beneficiaries of your work.

I feel most comfortable when I'm going along with the majority, so tell me why your product or service is already mainstream, or how your product or service is similar to something that is mainstream.

If you're presenting your work or solution to someone who you suspect is mostly influenced by social proof, then provide all the reasons everybody else loves your work.

The key point to remember here is that one type of information is not necessarily intrinsically better than another. So, if you are most moved by data and your business partner is most moved by anecdotes, you shouldn't just think, "Anecdotes are dumb, so I'm going to give them data instead." No! Winning conditions is understanding, accepting, and appreciating differences and modifying our own deliveries to respect others. Give your colleague the anecdote if that's what they most prefer.

Let's consider an example to understand this concept better. Perhaps you're the hiring manager for an organization, and you want to encourage a candidate to accept your offer of employment. Here are some examples of information that you could provide to the candidate to motivate them to accept the position. If you suspect the candidate is most motivated by . . .

. . . anecdotal evidence, then: "John Smith was hired into this position two years ago. Have you heard of John? John learned so much in this position and was so highly respected that he went on to become the division manager. John ended up making a huge positive difference for our organization and this entire team. You could do this, too."

. . . data, then: "Two hundred candidates applied to this position, forty received interviews, and of all of them, we chose you. You are our top 0.5 percent."

. . . dollars, then: "We're offering you $X per year salary, plus $Y company contribution to your health, life insurance, and retirement plans. We also offer commuter benefits valued at $Z per year. Our total compensation package is extremely financially rewarding."

. . . expert authority, then: "Experts suggest that making a career move like this, at this point in your life, will result in the greatest positive impact to career progression."

. . . intuition/emotion, then: "You will absolutely love it here. My greatest concern is that if you turn down this offer, then you will deeply regret losing out on this opportunity."

. . . leader support, then: "I shared your profile with our CEO and they agree that you will make a great difference in our organization."

. . . outcomes, then: "I'd expect that if you come on board now and work hard over the next few years, you will be running this team in twenty-four to thirty-six months. You can expect your salary to increase 3 percent a year with sizable year-end bonuses included. If you decide against this position, you'd likely not see such growth in your current role."

. . . social proof, then: "Everyone who met you during your interview said you were the top choice. We all agree that you are the perfect candidate," or "There has been an over-whelming demand for this position—everybody sees it's open and wants it."

You can see how these statements are all quite different and support different viewpoints in different ways. Which is most influ-ential and motivating *to the candidate*?

A number of years ago, I was invited by my large global organization to participate in a women's leadership initiative that aimed to support the growth of women into the higher executive leadership roles. Part of the initiative included pairing each female executive with a high(er)-level sponsor. A sponsor is someone who advocates for your success and champions your professional growth by sharing their own personal networks and using their influence within these networks to help you progress. Those of us in the program were able to select our preferred sponsors from a list of approximately forty executives who were willing to take on a sponsorship role. I remember looking over the list and deciding that I was going to select the highest-level sponsor possible—our chief executive officer. The only problem was that the CEO wasn't on the list.

I gave a great deal of thought to what might motivate the CEO to be my sponsor. Although I had never met him, I thought outcomes motivation ("here's how you will eventually benefit from this relationship") might be right. I wrote him a short email and suggested that it would look positive for our organization if even the CEO was participating in the women's leadership program. Furthermore, because my role involved a forward-facing, nontraditional focus, his pairing with me would further position our company in a forward-facing, positive light. The CEO of that forty-thousand-employee company wrote me back in less than five minutes. My pitch was spot-on. Two days later I was sitting in his office.

Ultimately, the CEO did not act as my sponsor because of some unrelated timing and business issues. But nonetheless, he invited me for a meeting every month or two after that to find out what projects I was working on and to ask how things were going. I may not have secured a sponsor, but I secured an ally. Those are winning conditions.

Now, there are a few situations in which delivering your work using your colleague's preferred motivator might not be appropriate. First, it's inappropriate to use your colleague's motivator if the message is unreasonable or untrue. For example, you shouldn't fake an expert just to trick someone. You shouldn't claim that your leader supports your work if they do not. You shouldn't create false narratives to manipulate someone. You always want to ensure that the information you're providing is accurate and you remain ethically strong.

Second, business rules may require a specific kind of information, and in this case, you shouldn't just ignore the rules (or implied rules). For example, maybe your colleague really only cares about the social proof (what everybody else thinks), but dollars or data are traditionally required or expected. In this case, you should provide dollars or data, but you can go ahead and back up that information with the social proof.

Lastly, there are times when the expected norms might be out of date, or times when providing work in a particular way makes you feel uncomfortable or feel like you aren't being true to yourself or your beliefs. This can happen when we feel pressure to be too accommodating, to go along with potentially outdated social norms just to fit in, or to put other people's needs above our own to the detriment of ourselves or others. In these types of situations, it's not necessary to acquiesce in order to please a potentially outdated mindset. For example, you may wish to use gender-neutral pronouns for yourself and/or others, even if this is nontraditional in your environment.

The takeaway of all of this is that you want to be flexible in modifying your messaging, in order to maximize the chances of being heard and valued by others. But you also want to respect the company's rules while remaining ethically strong and true to yourself and your beliefs (see Chapter 11 for more about the importance of ethics in winning conditions).

GROUP MOTIVATIONS

What if you are not presenting to an individual, but instead, to a group of people with varying and multiple perspectives? Well, then you will want to hit on varying and multiple angles. It's an interesting exercise to listen thoughtfully to well-constructed political speeches, as highly skilled politicians (or their highly skilled speech-writers!) generally use each of the above tactics to ensure they appeal to all people. You'll hear concrete facts and figures supporting the suggested approach (data driven), and you'll hear how Mary Smith from Iowa benefited from this approach (anecdotal), and you'll hear about how the majority of a particular group or demographic believes in this approach (social proof), and you'll hear about the generals and heads who are backing this as the best approach (expert authority), and you'll hear about the expected result of this approach (outcomes), and you'll also hear some strongly worded points that make you feel safe or happy or angry (intuition/emotion).

Recently I was engaged in a consulting project for a company that was reviewing its financial policies in order to best focus its investment strategy. Part of the project included a conference call with various stakeholders to gain feedback on current and potential future plans. I had just written this chapter of my book, and I chuckled a bit when I heard the call mimic exactly what I had just written. One stakeholder wanted to know what the investment managers suggested (expert authority). Another stakeholder asked about the range of investment returns under various scenarios (dollars). Another asked what strategies are used by similar organizations (social proof). Another compared the situation to organic farming and theorized how the farmer might react under different scenarios (anecdote—and yes, this actually happened!). Another asked for the number of years that the organization had maintained the current strategy (data). That conference call clearly illustrated the need for providing varied perspectives within a diverse group in order to ensure your full audience best receives your message.

I even provided varied perspectives when I played *Survivor*. On the last day of the game—day thirty-nine—the final three (sometimes two) players that are left in the game will pitch their value to the jury. The jury is comprised of eight to ten players who were most recently voted out of the game, and this jury chooses the winner of the season from these remaining three (or two) players. As one of the final three players in the game, I remember trying to touch on varying perspectives when giving my final speech to the jury. I said each of the following quotes during *Survivor*, season 35, episode 14: "Million Dollar Night." Can you identify which perspectives I'm addressing as I make my pitch for the million-dollar prize?

1. "I was terrified when the challenges started. I was not allowed to play sports as a kid. [. . .] I threw up on the deck on the first challenge because this was the one thing that I was so scared of."

2. "I'm really proud that there have been 258 female contestants on *Survivor* and there are now only four that have won four individual immunities, and I am one of them. And then I also got two individual rewards and the secret advantage for the final Tribal, at almost fifty years old."

3. "All moms are heroes because they put other people before themselves. They don't even stop and think. They put themselves on the line every day. Yes, not like a firefighter or a marine, but it is with great love and no thought that they get in there and do whatever they have to do for their kids."

Here, I hit on three perspectives (anecdotes, data, and emotion). In your work meetings, you also may only want to hit on a few. Why not all? First, you may not have time to appeal to every possible perspective when you're presenting your product or service in a business meeting. But second, and possibly more importantly, if you aren't speaking to a large group, then you don't want to risk boring or aggravating your colleagues with potentially useless motivations that are irrelevant to the attendees. So spend some time in advance of your meetings consciously thinking about which perspective(s) will best appeal to your audience. Then figure out what information you can provide that will support the preferences.

Sharing varied perspectives during the final tribal council on *Survivor*, season 35, episode 14: "Million Dollar Night." Image courtesy of CBS.

What do you do if you have absolutely zero idea which type of information would most appeal to your audience? Well, you could observe your colleagues during some other interactions to see what styles seem to be most effective. Listen to the information they share to identify what they view as important. Do you hear them sharing a lot of anecdotes with other colleagues, or talking frequently about the financial impacts of their work? Maybe they often speak about how they feel, or their eyes light up when they quote expert research, or perhaps they end each email with "Let me speak with my supervisor." Pay attention to clues in the language they use to help you assess their motivations. You could also try a few different styles out and see if any are more effective than others. Or you could transparently share the ideas in this book with your colleague. Tell them that you're working toward being more effective in your interactions and you'd like to know which type of information is most impactful and preferred.

Ultimately, learning to present your work according to the style or perspective of your business partner will create a better chance of success and collaborative outcomes. But let's take this idea even further. Besides thinking about *what* information to provide to support your work, you also want to think about *how* to provide this information.

HOW TO SHARE IT

Back in the early 1990s, when I was working in that first actuarial consulting role at Kwasha Lipton and trying to find my way out of the shadows, I began to closely pay attention to different work styles and behaviors. Our firm was structured such that different teams worked on projects for different clients, so I was on one team for Client A projects, another team for Client B projects, another team for Client C projects, and so forth. Each of these client teams was managed by a different partner. And each of the partners wanted the same thing—results. It might be valuation results, or required contribution results, or results to be entered on a government filing. But essentially, the partners all wanted results done right. And since we were all actuaries, everybody wanted the data. Not an anecdote, not our CEO's endorsement, not an emotional plea. Show me the numbers. I knew exactly *what* to provide.

But I thought there might be more to learn here, and so I carved out just a little bit of time and consciously looked. I noticed that my different managers (the partners) had differing work styles. And even though they were all asking for same thing—results—they wanted these results provided in different ways. The *how* varied. Here's what I mean by that:

▶ One of my managers, Frank, was **bottom-line oriented**. When I provided results to him, he wanted the answer. Only the answer. I'd walk into his office and say, "Here is the answer. Let me know if you'd like the background." And then I would turn around and walk right back out of his office as quickly as I'd arrived.

▸ Another one of my managers, Linda, was **process oriented.** When I provided the results to her, she wanted more than the results—she actually wanted to see the process. I would tell her, "First I did this. Then I did this. Then I did this. This is the answer based on those steps. And here is the documentation of that entire process and the results."

▸ Others were more **group oriented** and wanted to understand that the results had been vetted and checked and approved through the group channels. Back then we used to do this thing we called "dotting," which meant that whenever a number was checked and approved, the reviewer would put a little pencil dot next to it. So with my group-oriented managers, I'd make sure I included all the ways the results had been dotted and by whom.

▸ Others were more **report oriented** and sought written proposals that detailed the benefits and drawbacks of the results, various internal and external considerations, and potential or probable outcomes. I would share written proposals with these partners, indicating how my results moved us closer to our ultimate goals.

And I found that I had a great deal of success with this strategy. Because I not only gave my managers the information that they wanted (data-driven results) but also provided this information *in the way that they most wanted to receive it,* they highly appreciated my contributions. I began quickly advancing through my career.

What would be the consequences of a mismatched *how?* I've seen situations where someone asks for results thinking they're going to get a fast, easy, one-line, back-of-the-envelope response. Three weeks later they're presented with a full PowerPoint deck and five supporting white papers as backup. Yikes. I've also seen the converse, where someone asks for results, expecting a thoughtful and thorough reply, only to be presented with a brief idea presented in ten words or less that hasn't been double-checked. Double yikes. In each of these cases, the audience probably won't appreciate the work as much as if it had been delivered in the way they expected. They might not value or pay attention to it like they could, or should. They might not value or pay attention to *you* like they could, or should. So take a moment to understand the preferred *how*.

Here's another example. At one point in my career, I became consciously aware of the length and style of a typical executive-level email within my organization. In that organization, and at that time, I noticed that as people moved into higher levels, their emails became shorter and shorter. I suspected that the executives were bombarded with higher volumes of email traffic as they advanced through their careers, so brevity became not just a preference but a necessity. Typically when they'd correspond, they'd include one or two sentences, no greeting, no closing. So I began to correspond in the exact same way. My emails to the executives became one or two sentences, no greeting, no closing. And I found that because I was corresponding in the way that was most impactful to these execs, my emails began to be read. I began to develop traction. The response rate improved. This was a detail that mattered. I had gotten the *how* just right.

My sister Ellen was an early reader of this manuscript, and she nonchalantly shared the ideas in this chapter with her son during a short car ride. Ellen later learned that my nephew used these ideas to convince his dad to purchase him new ski boots. Apparently my nephew gave some thought as to *what* and *how* to pitch his case to best appeal to my brother-in-law. He prepared and delivered an actual proposal, including all the points that he knew would be meaningful to his dad, and it worked!

In the next chapter, we'll continue down this path of recognizing and matching perspective, but we'll move beyond the information you deliver to cover technical versus nontechnical language. We'll also consider how to best use your language to influence other people to adopt your ideas.

CHAPTER 5

MATCH COMMUNICATION STYLES

I live in a fairly rural area of New Jersey. Believe it or not, New Jersey is not all highways and power plants. We actually have some beautiful farmland and green acres (hey, that's why we're the Garden State!). Homeowners in my town do occasionally lose a donkey or a cow, and then there are some pretty funny Facebook posts about a found donkey. But I digress . . . Living in this rural town also means that we have far too many problems with phone lines, internet, and cable. Massive trees that line the back roads seem to fall down every time the wind blows, taking out the lines and knocking out the cable. Older wiring is common and frequently breaks down, so we often enjoy static or interference or shorts. But regardless of the reason, the important part of my story is what happens once the cable is out—I'm rewarded with a home visit from my cable provider.

My assessment of a successful visit from the service technician of course starts with "Did they fix my cable?" but a big part of it also includes, "How aggravated did I become in the process?" You see, nothing is more irritating to me than when a service tech tries to razzle-dazzle me. I know nothing about cable. Heck, I hardly know where the modem is. Or even what a modem is. And then I get a tech who likes to use big words and talk all technical, and I have no idea what they're asking me. And I'm trying to comply, really, I am, but I'm confused and then frustrated and darn it, "What are you talking about?!" Please don't razzle-dazzle me with the cable. Please. It's just not my style.

Every once in a blue moon, I'll get the kind of service tech who suits me—they describe everything in a way that I can understand. I love that. They'll tell me to "Look for the little black box the size of a shoebox that has five blinking red lights" instead of directing me to some apparatus I've never heard of. They'll explain in nontechnical language exactly what they're doing without making me feel like I'm clueless. They don't try to impress me with fancy talk, because they recognize that I'm not a customer who needs it. In fact, I need the opposite of that. I need simple and basic. This service tech gets five stars, and I actually answer the telephone survey to rate them five stars because they make me so happy.

I think you can see where this is going. When you're interacting with other people in the workplace, you need to figure out who wants to be razzle-dazzled, and who wants the opposite of that. Some people prefer a highly complex and academic presentation—they like to think hard and sound smart. Others prefer a plain bread-and-butter-type approach—simple language, simple explanation. Maybe your colleague is somewhere in between. And just like my favorite service techs, you'll want to change up your communication to fit the person with whom you're talking. You'll find that there are times when the razzle-dazzle is appropriate and times when it's not necessary. Are you presenting to a formal group, or chatting in the coffee room? Will big words or little words be more valuable to this audience and this situation? Please don't try to impress everyone all the time with fancy talk just to sound smart. Instead, you may just end up annoying people.

I know a manager who every day learns a new Word of the Day. These words are not usually widely known or understood—words like *gloze* or *farrago* or *assuetude*. Then each day he'll try to use this new word ten or more times during regular conversations or presentations. He'll just throw in the word as if everyone around him knows exactly what he's talking about. He doesn't flinch or explain it or otherwise let on that it's a weird word. It's super that he's having fun and improving his vocabulary. Plus, he sounds really smart. But nobody has any idea what he means. And so, his audience is generally left feeling confused and exasperated. (I almost wrote here that his audience was frustrated by his perceived *aristophrenia*, but then I thought, nah, better not.)

Winning conditions is not confused and exasperated. Instead, it's inspired and understood.

We've already learned the value of observing alternate perspectives and delivering the right information in a way that will be most motivating to our business partners. Now we're going to explore a nuance of that delivery and talk specifically about the words that we use to be most influential, inspiring, and understood. We'll explore different levels of technicality (the razzle-dazzle . . . or not), including how the approach may differ depending on audience or application. Then we'll move into one specific application where the words we use definitely matter—when we're encouraging change or the adoption of our work or ideas.

WHY WE USE HIGHLY TECHNICAL LANGUAGE

Language is a beautiful thing. Most concepts can be expressed in a myriad of ways, with varying words, phrases, forms, and complexities. Poetry, song lyrics, and prose can all offer unique perspectives on even simple concepts like greeting a loved one or dancing. Nathaniel Hawthorne wrote, "Words, so innocent and powerless as they are, as standing in a dictionary, how potent for good and evil they become, in the hands of one who knows how to combine them."[5] Wow, this is powerful stuff—words can be used for good

---

5 Hawthorne, Nathaniel, *The Atlantic Monthly*, vol. 18, no. 110, December 1866.

or evil, depending on the intentions of "one who knows how to combine them." When you speak with your business partners, what is your intention? How will you combine them?

That sounds, perhaps, like a loaded question. Wouldn't everyone in the workplace have only the best of intentions? Don't we all prefer to communicate in a way that allows us to be well understood, valued, and respected? Consider my friend who every day learns a word of the day. He intends to be scholarly and diligent. He intends to stretch himself positively and share his learnings with others. But what generally results is exasperation. I'm sure he doesn't intend to frustrate his audience, but that's what happens. So let's explore a little bit what could happen when you use various nuances of language.

Technical language or *technical words* are the razzle-dazzle. When I say you are speaking in technical terms, I mean that you are using terms that people specific to your industry, role, level, company, or profession would be reasonably expected to know. These are terms or concepts that you had to learn as you learned your trade, role, profession, or company procedures. Therefore, people NOT specific to your industry, role, level, company, or profession might not understand your technical jargon.

Nontechnical language or *nontechnical words* are those that are not specifically related to your trade, level, role, company, or profession and can be well understood by the average person. Note: nontechnical language is not the same thing as unprofessional language.

Unprofessional language means speaking in a manner below the standards expected for that given profession. In all cases, our language in the workplace should remain proper, suitable, and highly professional.

So for example, the cable service tech might say:

Technical—"Please reconnect the coaxial cable."

Nontechnical—"Please locate the white cable with the round

metal end. Press it gently into the jack labeled 'TV in' and screw the metal end clockwise to secure the cable."

Unprofessional—"Hey, you, fix the f**king cable."

Winning conditions is accurately recognizing what your audience understands and prefers and speaking to that level of technicality. Now, there are several reasons people will use highly technical language when expressing themselves or explaining their work. Here are some completely appropriate reasons:

1. The speaker is engaging with others in their industry, level, role, company, or profession who all understand this language and prefer it;

2. The speaker is presenting at an event or engagement that requires it.

For example, if you're an auto mechanic and you're speaking to other professionally trained auto mechanics, then it makes sense that you call a car part by its technical name. You explain in technical words how to check, repair, or replace this part. If you're an academic presenting a thesis, giving a presentation to industry colleagues, or writing a white paper for industry peers, then you should comfortably go ahead and share your work in technical terms. In both of these examples, your audience of peers will expect you to use words that have been commonly learned by others in your industry, company, etc. They will understand you. It is fully appropriate. In fact, the use of nontechnical language in each of these cases might be inappropriate.

One of the real difficulties with technical language is that at times, it becomes an automatic default. Sometimes we learn a technical term and then use it so frequently in our work that it becomes commonplace. We forget that it's a technical term. We may find ourselves robotically using these technical words, even if everyone in the room doesn't understand them. In this case, we use the technical language because:

3. The speaker is so used to this language that they automatically assume everyone else understands all the terms, acronyms, references, and insinuations as well.

This would be a mistake. This isn't winning conditions.

I remember starting a new job, and during my first week I sat in a meeting where someone kept talking about "Pika." I knew exactly what Pika was—the fraternity guys I used to hang out with in college. They were members of the Pi Kappa Alpha fraternity, but we called them Pika for short. I wasn't sure why we were talking about these guys in an insurance setting. I knew it must be something else, but I was too embarrassed to ask. Later I found out that Pika was really PICA, and it stood for Prudential Insurance Company of America, DUH.

I shared this embarrassing story with an understanding friend who I knew would never laugh at me for being so foolish, and he laughingly shared his own. He was at a meeting when the presenter was going on and on about MMA. He, like me, knew exactly what that was—mixed martial arts. But he, like me, wasn't sure why they were talking about martial arts in a business meeting. Later he found out they were not saying "MMA" but instead "M&A," as in "mergers and acquisitions."

Here's the thing—both of us are smart people! We just didn't connect the dots. And sadly, both of us were too embarrassed to ask during the meeting itself what the speaker meant. Because we didn't understand the acronyms during the meeting, we missed a lot of great information that the presenter intended to share. It's like we were back in the third grade when the joke of the week was, "Psst! Your epidermis is showing."

So when you engage with your colleagues, if you plan to use any potentially confusing, new, or unknown terms or acronyms, then just pause for a minute and explain briefly. *"The PICA results—Pruden-tial Insurance Company of America—are listed here on page 2,"* or *"Mergers and acquisitions activity is listed here under M&A."* It only takes a moment and goes a long way to engage your audience. Your audience won't subconsciously feel like the uncomfortable and unknowing victim of a third-grade joke. Becoming consciously aware of the words that we're using—and simplifying our language as appropriate to our audience—is winning conditions.

Let's keep going. Sometimes people mistakenly use technical language because:

4. It's easier to use a technical term than to have to explain it in nontechnical language.

Let's face it—most of us like to be efficient. Why explain things in twenty words if we can explain the same thing in two? Sometimes it's hard to remember back to when we were learning a concept and we needed the nontechnical language, too. My hairdresser recently told me she was going to use a double process. My tax accountant asked about exemptions. The plumber said our water tank needed a new bladder. In each of these cases, I had to ask what all this meant. What's a double process? Please explain the exemptions. What's a bladder? It's not that I'm not smart, I'm just not a colorist, an accountant, or a plumber.

My profession—actuarial science—is known as a highly technical one. We actuaries love our technical terms. To us it's obvious what a p-value or standard deviation or valuation is. And these might be hard concepts to explain to others, so sometimes we won't even try. But we have to try. Explaining the concepts is winning conditions.

"I calculated the p-values for these variables. The p-value is . . ."
"I'm going to use a double process, which means . . ."
"The exemptions are . . ."
"The bladder is . . ."
Here's the thing—*every profession is a technical one.* Every

profession, level, and role has its own secret language. Take a minute and explain what you mean. Even if you're the service technician and it's super obvious to you what a coaxial cable is. If you explain it to me thoughtfully, without making me feel stupid, then I'll give you five stars on the postvisit telephone survey.

Which brings us to our next point: "Explain it to me thoughtfully, without making me feel stupid." Sometimes people use highly technical language because:

5. The speaker thinks that technical language makes them sound smart and they want other people to think they are smart. (The extreme version of this is when the speaker wants to feel smarter than the audience.)

This is part of what motivates my friend who learns a word of the day—he likes sounding smart. The truth is, sometimes it feels rewarding to speak with big words. We feel intelligent, competent, and capable. We want to instill a feeling of respect and admiration. But it's possible that this can backfire on us. If the level of technicality is inappropriate, then instead of being impressed, people may feel put off. They may think you sound condescending or unapproachable. They won't view you with respect, but instead they may view you with disdain. Sometimes your audience will simply prefer little words.

Remember, we are here defining technical language as "terms that people specific to your industry, role, level, company, or profession would be reasonably expected to know." If someone doesn't understand a term that you're using, then it's *your* responsibility to share its meaning. By explaining clearly what you mean, you will be increasing your own value. Confusing your audience is not increasing your value. So instead of telling his staff simply, "That's a farrago of excuses," my friend could say, "That's a farrago of excuses. It's a confused mixture, a hodgepodge, a mess. It's chaos. Let's try and make some sense out of that farrago—or mess—of excuses."

I've seen news blurbs that even after becoming a billionaire, Warren Buffett continued living in the house he purchased back in 1958 for around $31,000 (this would be the present-day equivalent of about $275,000). The fact is—everyone knows that Warren Buffett is rich. I suppose he never felt the need to live in a twenty-thousand-square-foot mansion to prove it. We can apply Buffett's cue to "talking smart." That is, in the same way you don't need to necessarily live in a big house for people to know that you're rich, you don't need to necessarily use big words for people to know that you're smart. Mostly, people just want to be able to understand you. Use big words because they are appropriate for your audience and application—not because you think they make you sound smart.

Lastly, sometimes people use highly technical language because:

6. The speaker wants to confuse their audience so that the audience doesn't ask certain questions or probe too deeply; or

7. The speaker doesn't care about the audience or care whether the audience understands.

These last two are clearly not winning conditions. There is no benefit here. Please, just don't do it. The last thing you want is for people to question your good intentions.

USING LANGUAGE TO PROMOTE A NEW IDEA

Now, consideration of technical versus nontechnical (or the amount of razzle-dazzle) isn't the only time we want to thoughtfully modify our language. One of the most prominent places that deliberate wording can make a huge difference in outcome is when you are seeking to influence or encourage a particular outcome—specifically, if you are pitching a new idea. You could be a physical therapist encouraging a new exercise to a patient, or a marketing manager trying to sell an innovative new campaign. You could be a technology expert promoting a new use of artificial intelligence to streamline records processing, or a pharmacist looking to improve your pharmacy's shift scheduling. You could be the cable technician encouraging me to use the new voice-activated remote control. The question is, when you're suggesting or promoting change, how do you best encourage your audience to say yes? Do you use the same talking points for all people, even though some people are inevitably more open to change and others are not? (Hint: no!)

It turns out that phrases that incentivize some people to embrace your work might incentivize others to reject it. To understand this better, let's take a look into a popular framework known as the *adoption curve*.

The adoption curve was originally developed in the mid-1950s by three professors out of Iowa State University—Joe Bohlen, George Beal, and Everett Rogers—to categorize farmers' tendencies when purchasing hybrid seed corn. The framework they developed has since proven itself to be largely universal: people are not all equally accepting of new ideas. That is, some people are naturally more open to adaptation and innovation than others. The adoption curve has since been successfully applied to many different fields beyond agriculture, including marketing, technology, social work, communication, public health, and criminal justice.

The adoption curve segments people into distinct groups based on their willingness to accept new technology, ideas, or innovations. The segments (innovators, early adopters, early majority, late majority, and laggards) were named by Bohlen, Beal, and Rogers, and these same labels are still formally used today. I'll explain the adoption curve segments first using the technical labels and then with nontechnical, colloquial descriptions so this is easier to understand. As we move through the segments, remember that one group isn't necessarily better or worse than another. These are simply different ways to embrace new ideas.

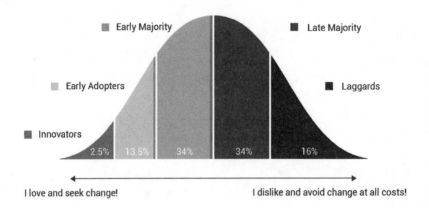

Early Majority

Late Majority

Early Adopters

Laggards

Innovators

2.5% 13.5% 34% 34% 16%

I love and seek change!   I dislike and avoid change at all costs!

Innovators are the smallest group. They love change and seek change! They are the risk seekers who are out front pulling for change. They are the first out of the gate, willing to try something new with little, if any, prompting needed. These people like to experiment and push forward with the latest and greatest products and services.

Early adopters are a larger group than the innovators but still only about an eighth of the population. They, too, like to get out in front and try new ideas, but in a slightly more careful way. They might want a few good reviews first before they will accept the new idea. Once they accept the idea, they become the opinion influencers leading the change.

The **early majority**, roughly a third of the population, feels comfortable adopting ideas only once there is strong evidence of their benefit. These are generally practical, cautious users who like things that have already been tested and approved by a few others. Note that while the early majority is slower to come on board than the early adopters, they still are accepting of change more quickly than the average.

The **late majority**, also a third of the population, agrees to a new idea or innovation when the majority of others are already using it. Sometimes we say they come on board after the *tipping point,* which is the point at which the new idea has been adopted by so many people that it's now not only significant, but often it's also irreversible. These people are more conservative and more skeptical of new ideas. They like to do a great deal of research before jumping on board. In fact, often the late majority will adopt strictly because of peer pressure.

Laggards are the slowest, or the most resistant to change. They avoid it whenever possible. Laggards generally will come on board only after the idea has become completely mainstream. In fact, often they are so fixated on the traditional past methods, and so risk averse, that they may actually come on board when the idea or innovation is already obsolete—or they might never adapt at all.

Here is a nontechnical way to think about willingness to accept change, based on the adoption curve model. Note that for ease of understanding I've combined innovators and early adopters into one segment.

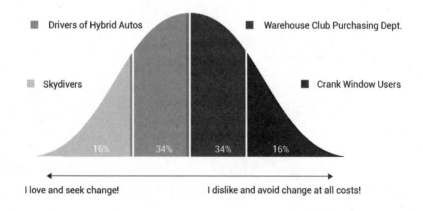

74

On the left are the **skydivers**. They love change and seek change! The airplane door opens and they jump. No holding back. They just go. They are the brave, the bold, and the fearless. Others might say they are the reckless, the wild, and the uncontrolled. The skydivers are willing to try something new with little prompting and often become the forward-thinking opinion influencers.

Slightly less risky are the **drivers of hybrid automobiles.** Hybrids, which operate on both gas-fueled internal combustion engines and battery-driven electric motors, have been tested and improved repeatedly over two decades, yet they still account for the minority of vehicles on the road. Hybrid owners are certainly in the early majority, but not because anything is particularly cutting-edge. These people are practical, careful, and cautious—but also forward-thinking and adaptable.

Then we have the **warehouse club purchasing department**. Warehouse clubs are massive retail stores that offer a limited selection of bulk items at deep discounts. The discounts are available because the stores turn over large volumes of goods. Thus, the purchasing departments for warehouse clubs (also known as "the people who decide what products to sell") would necessarily source well-tested products that are already used by the majority of consumers. Low risk and mainstream is the goal.

The most risk averse are those on the right—the people who avoid change at all cost. A friend told me a story once about their grandmother, who struggled with buying a new car because every model now included power windows, and she only wanted the old-fashioned manual window crank (hence, **crank window users**). Their grandmother also refused to use a cell phone because it didn't have a cord that connected the phone to the wall. People who insist on manual window cranks and corded phones are incredibly resistant to change. Maybe they are fearful of it, or don't understand it, or are simply proud traditionalists who will always think the old way is better.

* * *

Now, here is why this framework is helpful in creating winning conditions. Recognizing your audience's predisposition toward change will help you to showcase your idea or change in a way that is most incentivizing—or least intimidating—to your audience. Keep in mind that one segment of the adoption curve isn't necessarily better or worse than another—each is simply a different way to embrace new ideas.

▸ If you suspect that you're working with a **skydiver**, then phrases like "brand-new," "never been done before," and "cutting-edge" (if true) will motivate them to consider and value your work or ideas. Remember, skydivers love to get out in front of every new idea and embrace the idea before it becomes mainstream. So identify and highlight the aspects of your work that are innovative and exciting. Talk about the aspects that will "beat the competition" and "lead a change." If you instead lead with its mainstream aspects, you may have already bored them, and your work may be less appreciated.

▸ If you suspect you're working with a **hybrid driver**, then make sure to provide success stories and evidence of effectiveness. Share aspects that are "ahead of the curve but well tested," and encourage your colleague to "get on board before this is fully mainstream." If you pitch your work to a hybrid driver by suggesting something has never been done before, or that everyone else is already doing it, then your work may not be as readily accepted.

▸ If you suspect you're working with the **warehouse club purchasing department**, then share aspects of your work that have already been successfully adopted in mainstream areas. Use phrases like "widespread use" or "widespread benefit" to incentivize this group.

Promoting your work with the aspects that are "cutting-edge" and "leading the change" might discourage this audience from accepting it.

▸ If you suspect you are working with a **crank window user**, then go slowly, explaining things clearly and in simple terms. Understand potential apprehension and be patient. Remember that phrases like "we've never done this before" or "this is a brand-new innovation" can sound off-putting to those who are less comfortable with change. For them, what they already know or do has advantage over most other alternatives. They may actually look for reasons to reject your idea. Try and find some similarities to what is currently being done so the new idea is more palatable. Remember that you're already an expert in whatever it is that you're offering. You're already comfortable with it—your colleague may not be.

Now, in order to change your language based on where your audience falls on the adoption curve, you'll need to first place them on the adoption curve. It doesn't need to be exact. Are they more apt to innovate? Or more apt to use caution? Note that you are considering their *mindset* toward innovation, NOT their initial level of knowledge or their initial circumstances. For example, an organization might have an innovative mindset but be limited by old technology. In this case, even though they're operating with obsolete technology, if the *mindset* is innovative then you should lean toward talking points like "brand-new," "never been done before," and "cutting-edge."

Some theorists suggest that people are automatically directed into adoption curve segments based on age, social class, financial stability, and education. The thinking is that younger ages and higher levels of education and financial stability enable people to be more risky, therefore automatically labeling them skydiver or hybrid vehicle driver. They suggest that older, less educated, and less financially secure individuals would necessarily be the more risk-averse warehouse purchasers or crank window users. But while these factors may influence some people's comfort with risk, I don't agree that you should unilaterally assume a particular predisposition toward change based only on demographics.

It has been my experience that one's willingness to accept change could differ depending on the application. I personally am a skydiver in my career, using cutting-edge advanced analytics to improve decisioning and process flow within organizations. But I'm the warehouse purchasing department with my own personal technology—it takes peer pressure and widespread use before I'll update my own smartphone.

Overall, you want to remember that the language that incentivizes you may not necessarily be the language that incentivizes your business partner. What makes sense to you may not be what makes sense to them. Just like I prefer when the service tech speaks to MY level of comfort with advancements in cable technology, your customers, clients, and colleagues want you to speak to THEIR level of comfort with whatever you are offering.

Communication can make all the difference in achieving success, and that means communicating in a way that resonates with your audience. In the next chapter, we'll take this idea even further. Beyond modifying our phrasing depending on their levels of technicality and willingness to adopt change, we also want to consider whether our audience is currently satisfied or dissatisfied with the current state.

CHAPTER 6

RESPECT THE CURRENT STATE

On December 20, 2017, at exactly 7:19 p.m. Pacific Standard Time, I lost $900,000. After thirty-nine days of a cutthroat, difficult, draining, lonely, and painful game, and then 223 days of torturous waiting to find out the result during a live broadcast, my dreams were crushed. I lost to the marine. I watched his family rush onstage to celebrate with him during the live reunion show, while mine stayed planted in their chairs in the audience. I watched the fans and the press wrap him in love. I read countless media articles celebrating his heroic win. I was just second place. I was not the sole survivor. I did not win.

People still tell me that they are so disappointed. And that gives me some comfort.

On December 20, 2017, at exactly 7:19 p.m. Pacific Standard Time, I won $100,000 and the joy of knowing that I lived a dream. A dream! I might not have been the sole survivor, but after thirty-nine days of an epic, once-in-a-lifetime, spectacular adventure, and then 223 days of edge-of-my-seat waiting to find out the result during a live broadcast, I was finally complete. I came in second place! SECOND PLACE! I could see my family in the audience during the live reunion show, their hearts bursting with love and pride for all that I had accomplished. The fans and the press wrapped me up in love. Countless media articles celebrated my heroic run. I might not have been the sole survivor, but I did not lose. Oh no, I won plenty.

People still tell me that they are so disappointed. And that makes me frustrated.

So which is it?

As we now know, winning conditions is communicating in a way that will best resonate with your audience. In this situation, "I'm so disappointed" could either provide great comfort or great frustration. Most people don't stop to consider my feelings on this event before blurting out their own. I get that all the time—from not only fans, but also from friends, acquaintances, colleagues, community members, and even family. I know that a lot of people are so disappointed, and I'm sorry that you feel that way. But my reality is the second version of the story. I feel insanely blessed and happy that I had a chance to live this dream. It truly was a dream. Yes, I know I didn't win, but I came in SECOND PLACE!

Second place is obviously far better than anyone thought I'd ever do. When I told my plumber that I was on the upcoming season of *Survivor*, he shook his head and confessed, "I won't tell anyone because I don't want to be embarrassed when you're voted out first." This was a common sentiment. Several people close to me confided, "Well, at least we won't have to watch too much of the season, because we can bail after you get voted out." The joke's on them— they got stuck watching the whole season. Nope, I'm not disappointed. I'm thrilled. I'm thrilled at how well I did. I'm thrilled that I got a chance to play this great game. I'm thrilled that so many fans wrapped me up in love and to this day tell me that I'm their favorite player, or tell me that I inspired them to be a better person, or thank me for letting them know that the actuarial profession exists because now they want to be an actuary.

I'll tell you what does disappoint me—the fact that other people are disappointed. That makes me sad and frustrated. I'm sorry that second place is not good enough for them. I'm sorry that even with my great run, I am not good enough for them. Because that's how they make me feel when they say that. What I'd really love to hear from them is any of the following:

I loved watching you play!
You crushed those challenges!
I am so proud of you.

But I know deep down they aren't trying to be mean—they're trying to show me their loving support—and I understand why we have a disconnect happening here. This happens in the workplace all the time—too often—and can be the source of a great deal of conflict and even lost business. The disconnect (disagreement? error? aggravation?) can be explained by understanding what I call the *current state of contentment*, and it considers whether your audience is starting from a place of satisfaction or dissatisfaction. Let me explain.

SATISFACTION VERSUS DISSATISFACTION

Back in 1959, a psychologist named Frederick Herzberg wanted to learn more about what motivated people in the workplace. So he created a study and interviewed workers about their good and bad experiences at work. The questions were mainly open-ended—for example, he would ask them to describe situations in which they felt good about their jobs and in which they felt bad about their jobs. By understanding what made people happy (satisfied) and unhappy (dissatisfied) at work, he was hoping to better understand how to increase satisfaction and motivation in the workplace. We usually think about satisfaction and dissatisfaction like this, as a continuum:

Becoming more satisfied (moving to the right) is the same as becoming less dissatisfied. Becoming less satisfied (moving to the left) is the same as becoming more dissatisfied. But what Herzberg found was surprisingly different from this standard expectation. Herzberg learned through his research that workers' satisfactory experiences were based on one set of factors, and dissatisfactory experiences were based on an entirely different and separate set of factors.

▸ **Satisfaction** seemed to come from factors related to the work itself. Workers gained satisfaction from things like high performance, increased responsibility, appropriate recognition, opportunity for growth, opportunity for promotion/advancement, a sense of achievement, and meaningfulness of work.

▸ **Dissatisfaction** seemed to come from the workplace environment. Workers were dissatisfied when they had to endure things like poor workplace conditions, adverse or difficult relationships with colleagues, ineffectual company policies, low or uncompetitive salary, inferior benefits, and inadequate security.

The study findings suggested that because satisfaction and dissatisfaction are based on entirely different influences, they do not actually exist on a continuum. Instead, *they act independently of each other.* It turns out the graphic should not be continuous, but should instead be disconnected, like this:

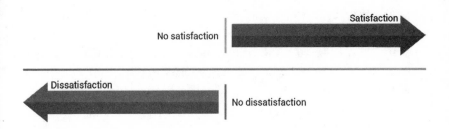

We can therefore conclude the following:

▶ Dissatisfaction is not the opposite of satisfaction. The opposite of satisfaction is no satisfaction. This means that if I am currently satisfied, and you take away my satisfaction, then I am now no longer satisfied. It does not, however, mean that I have necessarily become dissatisfied.

▶ The opposite of dissatisfaction is no dissatisfaction. This means that if I am currently dissatisfied, and you alleviate my dissatisfaction, then I am now no longer dissatisfied. It does not, however, mean that I have necessarily become satisfied.

▶ An increase in satisfaction is not the same thing as a decrease in dissatisfaction. So if I am satisfied and you do something to make me more satisfied, that's not the same thing as saying that you made me less dissatisfied.

▶ A decrease in dissatisfaction is not the same thing as an increase in satisfaction. If I am dissatisfied and you do something to make me less dissatisfied, that's not the same thing as saying that you made me more satisfied.

Essentially, inspiring your business partners (moving them from satisfied to more satisfied) requires a different approach than appeasing them (moving them from dissatisfied to less dissatisfied). In both cases you will aim to move right on the arrow diagram, but the words you use to do that will be quite different and will align with the arrow on which your audience starts. Because the starting point is key, I like to think of this idea as current state of contentment. What is the current state? Let's speak to that. Understanding the current state of contentment, and managing your delivery to that current state, is winning conditions.

INSPIRING OR APPEASING

We've already learned that different people have different points of view, attitudes, positions, and perspectives, because they have different roles, backgrounds, interests, personalities, experiences, training, and education. This means that their view may differ from your view, though it doesn't make their view any better or worse than yours. As we move through this chapter, remember that the current state of contentment considers how *your audience* feels, even if their view is different from yours. If you aren't sure, then ask.

How are you feeling about this?

It's the same concept as *"What did I miss?"* You're asking for information that will enable you to deliver a better work product or a better solution. Your pitch for your service, product, or idea will change depending on if your audience's current state of contentment is satisfaction or dissatisfaction.

If your colleague is currently satisfied, then you want your work, product, or service to make them even more satisfied.

Recognize and explicitly address that they're currently satisfied. Explain how your work or idea will make them more satisfied. You can use inspirational phrases like:

"This is excellent. Let's keep moving in this direction."
"You're already adding a great deal of value. This idea can help create even more value."
"I see you're in a good place, I can help make this even more satisfying."

You don't want to insinuate that your colleague is currently dissatisfied, as that may come off as insulting. Avoid phrases that seek to appease, like:

"I can fix this for you."

Basically, if your business partner is not unhappy, then don't insinuate that they are. Why not? Because this will cause your business partner to assume that *you don't understand the current state*, therefore they may also assume that your work, product, or solution might not be appropriate. Remember, the satisfaction/dissatisfaction relationship is not a continuum—these are separate and independent. A reference of dissatisfaction made to someone who is currently satisfied is a mistake and sounds off-putting. One might even call it an insult.

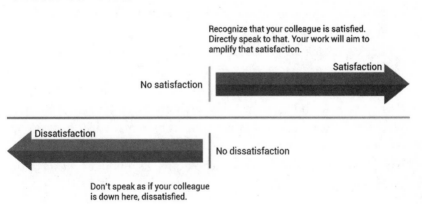

I'll give you a simple example.

I'm not one of those people who is bold enough to change my hairstyle or color regularly. I admire the people who can easily move from long to short or blond to red. Not me. My hair is pretty much always the same, although every once in a while I'll try bangs, or layers, or highlights. I'm brave enough to try just subtle changes, not because I think my hair looked bad before, but because it might be fun to try something a little bit new.

And inevitably, someone will bust out with something like, "Oh my gosh, WHAT AN IMPROVEMENT."

This person means well, really, they do. They think they're giving me a wonderful compliment. But there is a subtle insinuation in this exclamation that my hair looked bad before. Perhaps what I heard is not the same as what they specifically said, but somehow this comment sounds to me like my hair used to look like hell and it's a good thing I changed it. The comment frustrates me because I liked my last hairstyle. I wasn't actually dissatisfied. I just decided I'd change it up a little bit. Saying simply, "Your hair looks wonderful," or just "I love the highlights" would have made a more positive impact. They could even be more direct in noting my prior satisfaction, with something like, "It's beautiful, and you're lucky you have options because your hair looks great both ways."

Let's go back to the example of people saying "I'm so disappointed" about my *Survivor* experience. This statement is an appeasing phrase, and if I were starting from dissatisfaction, then that phrase would give me comfort. But I'm not starting from a place of dissatisfaction. I'm starting from a place of satisfaction, so instead the phrase just makes me frustrated. It makes me feel bad about myself—I feel like people are disappointed *in me*. An inspiring comment would serve me better:

You showed me that it's never too late to go after my dreams!

I had so much fun cheering you on all season!
What a great run! That was incredible!

In one of my prior roles, I would frequently hear pitches from external consultants or vendors who wanted to tout their latest technology, methods, processes, and ideas, which they promised would revolutionize my organization's business. When I think back to whom we would hire, or whom we would dismiss, it often came down to the current state of contentment. You see, my team was well aware of our current state. In some areas we knew we performed well as compared to industry standard. Some things we knew needed improvement. So, for example, let's say that one of our known strengths was our speed of claims processing. We were proud of that. Imagine we interviewed two vendors who offered excellent innovation in claims processing technology. The first vendor said:

> "Your current claims processing is truly outstanding. You're already so far ahead of competitors. Our innovative claims processing solution can keep you ahead of the pack and ensure that your customers continue to be served in unsurpassed fashion. If you hire us, we will help you to keep your top ratings. We value the same strengths."

The second vendor said:

> "We have developed our innovative claims processing solution to solve many problems that organizations experience. We can help you fix your problems, too. We can help you improve your speed. We can help you to better serve your customers. We can help fix your customer satisfaction ratings. If you let us help you, then we can teach you to become number one in your space."

In this case, it's not difficult to see which vendor we would have invited back. The first vendor recognized our current state. They would have helped us gain more satisfaction from something that we already felt we were doing well. In contrast, the second vendor didn't understand us. We didn't need them to fix anything. Nothing was broken. We were already number one in our space. Frankly, they were low-level insulting us.

Remember, if your business partner is already satisfied, then you want to inspire them. You don't need to appease them, or *fix* something that they don't believe is currently broken.

Now let's talk about dissatisfaction.

If your customer or colleague is currently dissatisfied, then you want your work, product, or service to make them less dissatisfied.

Be empathetic and understanding about the fact that your business partner feels as if they're in a frustrating, substandard, or otherwise dissatisfactory situation. If your colleague is dissatisfied, then you want your work, product, or service to make them *less dissatisfied.* You can seek appeasement with phrases like:

"I'm sorry you're dealing with this. I'll help you change it."
"Let's work together to improve this."
"I have a solution that can help fix this."

You don't want to insinuate that things are great, or your business partner might assume you don't understand current state. Avoid inspirational phrases like:

"This is great. Let's keep moving in this direction."

Um . . . no. This direction is awful. Remember, your goal is for your colleague to feel your empathy and recognize that your work, product, or ideas will help make things better.

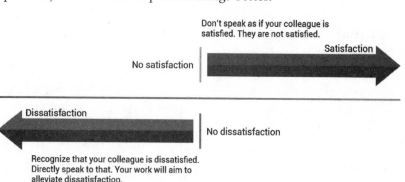

Now, if the situation is by all rational accounts in great shape, then you shouldn't lie and pretend it isn't. In fact, part of winning conditions is remaining ethically strong, and I'll discuss the importance of honesty and ethics further in Chapter 11. But you can modify your language to represent that you understand their truth. THEIR truth. For example, you shouldn't lie and say, "This is awful" if it isn't, but you could say, "I'm sorry this is frustrating for you. My work can help this situation become better for you."

A couple weeks ago, I was at the auto repair shop after my car's check-engine light came on. I've already driven my car over 180,000 miles, but a new car isn't in the budget with two—soon three—kids in college and all those tuition payments. While I received a decent payout of *Survivor* winnings, the more accurate statement is that Boston College received a decent payout of *Survivor* winnings! So alas, my old clunker remains in my garage. Anyway, I was devastated when I heard how many thousands of dollars it would cost to fix the problem. Instead of recognizing my despair and disappointment over the cost, and empathetically phrasing their response to alleviate my distress ("I'm sorry, I know it's a lot of money and this is really frustrating, but my team can get you back on the road safely"), the service person behind the counter laughed and said,

"Just buy a new car." Their lack of recognizing my current state of (dis)contentment only succeeded in causing me greater distress. They didn't understand me. They didn't understand my needs.

At one time in my career I was assigned to a temporary consulting project within a host organization that seemed to do little to discourage its quite toxic environment. During the course of the assignment, I noticed that one of the team managers regularly verbally degraded his team. Women in the office who weren't pregnant were asked why they wore maternity clothes. At one point, I was invited to share my highly technical work with a group of executives from other areas of the organization. When I walked in the room, I was grabbed around the waist, kissed right on the lips, and introduced with the not-at-all-amusing-and-in-fact-quite-inappropriate quip, "Aren't I so lucky I get to work with girls who look like this?" Yes, I reported the incident. No, nothing changed.

As you can imagine, my levels of dissatisfaction were maximized. Sure, this was a temporary assignment for me, but there were many permanent employees who suffered in that environment every day. They didn't necessarily have the option of moving to a different position, team, or employer. The working conditions needed a massive overhaul. The problem was, management didn't understand the magnitude of the dissatisfaction within the office. What we all needed and wanted to hear was any of the following:

"I'm sorry you're dealing with this. I'll help you change it."
"Let's work together to improve this."
"This is wrong. We have a solution that can help fix this."

But instead of alleviating dissatisfaction and correcting the office toxicity, management instead tried to boost satisfaction:

"We're distributing sizable year-end bonuses!"
"Here's an added responsibility! Here's a bigger team!"

"Here's another great project because you are doing such a great job!"

Those tactics failed. Eventually I requested to be reassigned—I simply couldn't take one more day in that environment. Many others resigned as well. We didn't need more satisfaction to make this work. We needed less dissatisfaction. (Side note: I've been told that in the years since, the organization has reorganized those areas and created a healthier environment.)

THINK ABOUT IT!

Here are some examples with differing slants toward the current state of contentment to help start you thinking about your own situation. If you are . . .

. . . a personal trainer, does your client want to stay healthy (currently satisfied) or lose weight (currently dissatisfied)?

. . . a loan officer, is your customer excited to finally be buying their dream home (currently satisfied) or are they devastated that they just experienced a catastrophic loss (currently dissatisfied)?

. . . a customer service representative, is your caller providing positive feedback (satisfied) or asking you to fix something that is troubling (dissatisfied)?

. . . new to your position, are you replacing someone who was competent or incompetent?

. . . a coach, is your team trying to continue their winning streak or turn around a losing streak?

Mishandling the current state of contentment can derail small projects and massive projects. It can leave employees feeling dissatisfied or cause their resignations. It's not difficult to change up your language based on the current state—and can completely change the outcome of your projects. Consider this.

"MANAGEMENT HAS DECIDED . . ."

These days, organizations across industries are increasingly using predictive analytics to solve complex business problems and streamline processes. Predictive analytics uses vast amounts of data and improved computing power to help make good decisions faster and with greater consistency than we humans can. At one point in my career, I became involved in a project that aimed to streamline an insurance application process. It was a multimillion-dollar project and the largest initiative the organization had undertaken in several years.

Historically, when someone applies for insurance, they complete an application and submit it to the insurance company. The application is received by underwriters, who review the information submitted and make a decision on coverage (accept or decline) and price. The underwriters' decisions are based on rules frameworks, but there is some subjective input as well. The more experienced underwriters are usually assigned to the more complex cases. Other cross-functional departments like actuarial and information technology are also usually involved, to provide historical data, pricing, and results to the underwriters to aid in their decision making.

Introducing a predictive model into an insurance process like this can streamline the entire operation. While a model may or may not necessarily make better decisions than a human, a human-plus-model combination can usually make better decisions than human-alone.

Now, months before I joined this project, management had hired external consultants to build the predictive model and then told the underwriters, actuaries, and IT something like this:

"After careful consideration, management has decided we are going to use a predictive model to improve the insurance application process. Please provide appropriate resources to the consultants who are building this model."

This sounds reasonable enough. I'm sure we've all been in situations where we were tasked to do something that management decided, simply because they decided it. So of course these teams outwardly said, "Okay." But when I came on board months later, I found that the model was being wholeheartedly rejected by the users. Underwriting, actuarial, and IT were throwing out roadblocks to completion every step of the way. And management had no idea why this was happening. But I did—and now you, dear reader, do, too.

Current state of contentment.

The problem here is nuanced language—management didn't recognize and explicitly address the teams' current state of contentment. Because of this, the teams became frustrated. They became adversaries, not advocates, and began to put up roadblocks. You see:

The **underwriters** felt they were already doing a great job selecting and pricing cases. Results were good, and goals were consistently met. They were starting from a place of satisfaction.

But the communication sounded to them like management was looking to fix something that was broken. The communication did not recognize a satisfactory starting point, explicitly address the underwriters' current value and great work, or inspire them further. Instead, it sounded like the model might *replace* them. This subtle communication issue caused friction. The underwriters felt underestimated and wronged. Satisfaction was reduced. And this situation undermined the project.

The **actuaries** had always been the data experts—they, too, were currently satisfied. They were proud of their consistently high level of contributions.

But the introduction of a consultant gave them the impression that management was unhappy with the actuaries' work, otherwise the external group would not have been secured. The actuaries felt underestimated and wronged. Satisfaction was reduced. Again, the subtle communication issue caused friction and undermined the project.

Information technology was already overwhelmed and overworked. They were stuck managing legacy computer systems held together with Band-Aid fixes. IT was dissatisfied.

To them, management did not recognize the current state. Instead, management just dumped another project into their laps. The introduction of yet another program to maintain added to their dissatisfaction. They felt frustrated and wronged. Dissatisfaction was amplified.

So subconsciously (or maybe consciously) these teams put up roadblocks. In each of these cases, the current state was not *explicitly recognized*. It was not *explicitly shared* how this work would improve the current state. And therefore the project broke down. What if, instead of saying "management has decided . . ." the management had instead implemented winning conditions? To create winning conditions in a situation like this one, a management team could:

Approach the underwriters. Explain that their excellent work has been noted, and management wants to concentrate their deep expertise on the most difficult and complex applications. A predictive model will be implemented to execute the easy stuff. The underwriters can spend their time on the more difficult and interesting applications. Get them excited about increasing their great value. Satisfaction is amplified.

Approach the actuaries. Explain that their vast expertise in the organization's data is critical to building a great model, so they are important to this process. Recognize their great work. Explain that a consultant was brought in because the actuaries are already working long hours and studying for exams—dumping more work on them would be unfair to them. Help them to be more satisfied.

Approach IT. Ask them for their opinions and expertise regarding the model. Tell them that you understand how frustrating it is to work with such old systems, so you want to engage them to ensure this model doesn't freeze up or slow down anything they use currently. Dissatisfaction is reduced.

We actually did ultimately change the conversation to reflect the above realignment of perspective and were able to get that model up and running. It ended up being a big success story for the organization.

Now that you've learned that satisfaction and dissatisfaction are separate and independent, think about your colleagues. Are each of them currently satisfied or dissatisfied? If you aren't sure, then ask them. Can you think of a way to articulate your work's value that will increase the satisfaction of your satisfied colleagues? Can you think of a way to articulate your work's value that will decrease the dissatisfaction of your dissatisfied colleagues? If you begin using these new perspectives and directly address the current state of contentment, then you will see a definite improvement in your outcomes.

Beyond improving communication and outcomes, there is yet another benefit of recognizing someone's current state of contentment, and this relates to correctly interpreting "no feedback." Let's check it out.

INTERPRETING THE NO-FEEDBACK SITUATION

Have you ever been in a situation when you worked hard on something but then received zero feedback? The situation often plays out like this: you spend a great deal of effort perfecting your work, and you're so proud of that work. You submit your work and then eagerly wait to hear how it is received. And then . . . nothing. *I'll wait a bit longer.* Still nothing. *Hmm. Did my manager like it? Not like it? Did I do a good job? A horrible job? Are they not saying anything because they're busy? Or was my work awful? Or do they not feel the need to provide feedback? Bueller? Bueller?*

I remember having a conversation with one of my colleagues a number of years ago, lamenting that my manager didn't give me feedback on a project. My manager generally loved my work and was highly appreciative and supportive. Whenever I gave them results or a report, they'd tell me all the things I'd done well. This time, I had expected them to be thrilled with the project I had completed and submitted, yet after a week, I still hadn't received any feedback, and this began to concern me. I shared these concerns with a trusted colleague. My colleague's response was interesting.

She remarked that she always preferred no feedback. You see, her manager was a nitpicker. Her manager was the kind of person who found something wrong with everything. Didn't matter what it was—too long, too short, too thorough, too brief, right method but wrong data, preferred a different chart, new labels, fewer billable hours, an email not a phone call, or a phone call not an email. Or maybe even—she'd finally submitted the perfect project but her manager would change two words on the cover letter just so that they could feel smarter and better than my colleague. That was her experience. So for her—well, no feedback was glorious! No feedback was actually quite a compliment!

Current state of contentment can provide some insight to these no-feedback situations. In general, colleagues who are typically satisfied will vocalize their satisfaction. When they are satisfied, they will let you know. So if you submit your work to someone who generally sits on the satisfaction line, then silence may indicate no satisfaction (this is bad). Alternatively, colleagues who are generally dissatisfied will vocalize their dissatisfaction. When they are dissatisfied, they will let you know. So if you submit your work to someone who generally sits on the dissatisfaction line, then silence may indicate no dissatisfaction (this is good). While only a loose rule of thumb, gleaning some insight into whether *no feedback* is a good thing or a bad thing can enable you to better gauge responses and better deliver your work. As we've already learned, people are not all the same—and so we can't expect them to respond similarly in similar situations.

The takeaway of this whole thing is that becoming mindful of the current state of contentment will help you better share your work's value and better understand its reception.

We're going to hit on one more set of ideas for understanding our audience before we then turn to a more internal focus. In the next chapter, we'll explore some more phenomena of our human brains. We'll learn how different kinds of predictable irrationality can affect our business partners' decisions about our work—and therefore impact our success. On to Chapter 7!

UNDERSTAND MOTIVATIONS FOR CHANGE

am a self-admitted superfan of reality TV. I love it all. My obses-sion began back in the spring of 1997. My husband and I had just been married, and we settled into a routine of watching TV instead of going out to dinner or even on vacation, because we were saving for a down payment on a house and simultaneously putting him through graduate school. We just didn't have the money to go out. And so, our typical after-work or weekend entertainment was inexpensive microwave popcorn and a television show on the couch.

One evening we stumbled upon the *Eco-Challenge*, a week-or-so-long grueling competition in which coed teams of four would traverse across more than five hundred kilometers of exotic terrain by trekking, rafting, climbing, mountain biking, kayaking, and hiking. The modest prize was simply a rebate of the $10,000 entry fee. Not all the teams would even finish. The Eco-Challenge was created and directed by Mark Burnett and released on Discovery Channel, and I was immediately hooked. I loved the adventure, the exotic locations, and the team dynamics. I remember trying to convince my husband that we should eat spaghetti every night for a year and use the grocery money that we'd save on plane tickets to the Eco-Challenge. I wasn't athletic enough to compete but assumed

I could at least volunteer to serve dinner at the teams' rest tent. (P.S. My husband didn't go for this idea.) I craved adventure desperately and thought that serving dinner to competitors would probably be the closest I'd ever come to experiencing a reality adventure competition myself. I thought Mark Burnett was probably the coolest and smartest and most creative person in the entire entertainment world, and I needed as much Mark Burnett TV as I could get my hands on.

He delivered. A few years later, in May of 2000, Burnett released another reality television program. This one was called *Survivor*, and I watched from the very first episode. I thought maybe—just maybe—I could do this one. My application went in the following summer, and while I waited for casting to call, I watched more. I needed more. I was fascinated.

I tuned in to *Big Brother*, filmed entirely in one secluded house in Los Angeles. I fell into *The Amazing Race*, which took racers and viewers across the globe. I watched singles finding love (and hopefully an engagement) on *The Bachelor* and, later, *The Bachelorette*. I rooted for my favorite boxers on *The Contender* and my favorite professionals on *The Apprentice*. I will even publicly admit that the *Real Housewives* franchise and *Rock of Love* had me hooked. I was obsessed with all of these. I learned that I didn't necessarily need the exotic locations of the *Eco-Challenge* or *The Amazing Race* to pique my interest, because the human dynamics and decisions that I saw play out in the other programs were equally compelling.

At times, I couldn't believe that people would behave in certain ways or make particular choices. Players sometimes seemed to me to be completely irrational. Why would they vote out this person when that person was a bigger threat? Why would they choose this Detour instead of the other Detour in the Race? Why would they put those two houseguests On the Block? Why does that suitor get a rose? Sometimes the decisions appeared to leave the decider in a worse situation. But I realized, this is all just typical human nature. Human nature is such that sometimes we behave in a way that leaves us in a suboptimal state.

You know why we do this? Yep—because we are humans and we have human brains. Remember: our incredible brains allow us to function, learn, remember, analyze, strategize, and feel. They allow us to think, care, consider, reflect, and reason. But our incredible brains also forget, err, mess up, and break down. Sometimes we make decisions that are irrational. And reality TV showed this clearly. I was compelled to watch, and understand, and dissect this human nature. It was a complete reality circus.

The workplace is its own reality circus, too, at times. I'd bet that you've seen decisions being made in your workplace that have left you wondering, "What on earth could they have been thinking? Why did they do that?!" or even, "Why wouldn't they do that?!" Winning conditions can help you to manage your interactions to promote optimal decision making.

In our journey so far, we've learned that our business partners should be reasonably open to change if it makes sense given past events and if it's supported by the current players. We've provided the evidence that is most compelling, and we've delivered that evidence in the most compelling way. We've appropriately inspired or appeased, with language that is technically appropriate and well understood. We've identified our business partners' predisposition toward change and adjusted our talking points accordingly. Shouldn't our business partners now automatically say yes? Is it possible that if we've done everything right, our business partners may still not accept our new ideas?

It turns out, in the same way that our predictably irrational human brains might sometimes become unintentionally blind to details that matter, we might also sometimes unintentionally make suboptimal decisions. We may suggest or take action when *inaction* is the better option; we may reject action when *action* is the better option. If we can better understand the biases that may lead to suboptimal decision making, then we can work to improve both our own decision making and the decisions of others. This will improve our outcomes, so let's explore.

THE STATUS QUO BIAS

Sometimes our brains fall into a decision-making trap known as the *status quo* bias. President Ronald Reagan once famously quipped, "That is a Latin phrase—status quo—for 'the mess we're in.'"[6] When describing this decision bias, he's exactly right. Status quo is a shortened form of the Latin phrase *status quo ante*, which translates to "the state existing before" or "the state in which before." Essentially, *status quo* means the current state or the previous decision. Accordingly, the status quo bias refers to an individual's disproportionate likelihood of preferring the current state (or previous decision) over all else. Think about those people who just love crank windows in cars. When we fall into the status quo trap (or mess), we actually look for reasons to do nothing, even if that means missing out on potential benefits.

There are a few theories about why the status quo bias exists:

Loss aversion—We may feel the pain of a loss as a stronger emotion than the pleasure of a gain. For example, I might feel extreme disappointment from losing ten dollars (ugh!!!) but only mild joy from finding ten dollars (oh, that's fun). Loss aversion causes people to do what they can to avoid a potential loss, even if this means forgoing a potential benefit. After many years of microwave popcorn on the couch, my husband and I started going out to dinner (but only occasionally!). When we go out, it's almost always to our favorite local restaurant. Whenever we go there, I order the same meal. Every time. Grilled salmon with mango salsa. It never changes. Why not? Loss aversion. Even though I *might* enjoy another entrée, I don't want to risk it. I'd rather forgo the benefit of a new, delicious taste in order to avoid the disappointment of potentially not enjoying my dinner at all. And yes, I know that my brain is acting irrationally when I do this.

---

6 Reagan, Ronald. "Address Before a Joint Session of the Tennessee State Legislature in Nashville." Nashville, Tenn., March 15, 1982.

It's the same way in the workplace. A colleague may forgo a wholly appropriate solution, process, change, or method in order to avoid a potential loss. (Note: This may be especially rampant in organizations where any type or measure of failure is extremely frowned upon.)

If you suspect that your colleague is irrationally maintaining the status quo because of loss aversion (when all rational considerations indicate action), then try this—instead of phrasing your product or service in terms of the potential benefits gained, share the potential losses that will result if your product or service is NOT used. Remember, the pain of loss is greater than the pleasure of gain. People are more likely to take an action if this action minimizes potential loss.

Instead of: "Use of this product will expand market share by 3 percent."
Try: "If you don't use this product, you'll lose 3 percent market share."

Instead of: "These exercises will help you feel better."
Try: "If you don't do these exercises, you will continue to experience chronic pain."

Instead of: "This update will move us ahead of the competition."
Try: "If we don't complete this update, we'll fall behind the competition."

Pointing out potential losses could initiate and encourage the rational, ideal, and optimal action that you seek.

Familiarity—We may believe that we prefer the current state simply because we are more familiar with it (more on this in Chapter 8). Change makes many of us uncomfortable, and in that mindset, any change from the current state is viewed as a loss. Therefore, we prefer to stick to the way things are right now. Familiarity is why my husband and I continue to eat out at our local restaurant. We're familiar with it; therefore, we believe it is our favorite. We know by name the owner, the bartender, the waitstaff, and the servers. We have our favorite table. Of course, I order my favorite entrée, along with my favorite wine. I prefer the things with which I'm more familiar. I view lack of familiarity as a loss. My human brain considers a different restaurant, with unfamiliar staff, menu, and wine list, to be a loss, simply because it is unfamiliar.

In the workplace, this is often why we interact with people we know instead of meeting new colleagues. It's why we've run the same programs for the past fifty years—sure, another way might be faster, but we like it this way. It's why a change of habits is off-putting. We resist action because it's easier to go with what we know. We're comfortable with what we know. Some would say that "The devil you know is better than the devil you don't." But what do you do when it's not?

If you suspect that your colleague is irrationally maintaining the status quo because of familiarity (when all rational considerations indicate action), then try to share as much information as you can about the "unknown" idea that you are recommending. Share this information as often as possible, using words that your colleague will easily understand. A new method or new information might not seem familiar if we hear it once, but hearing about or talking about concepts repeatedly will encourage familiarity. And then familiarity with the new idea or solution or concept will bring increased acceptance. It will no longer be strange, novel, or "the devil you don't [know]."

Omission bias—We may sometimes choose to do nothing over doing something, because we judge harmful *actions* more seriously than equally harmful *omissions*. Said differently, it may be preferable to make a mistake by doing nothing than to make a mistake by actively doing something wrong. Why? Making a mistake through action tends to leave us with a greater feeling of regret and responsibility than if we had made a mistake of inaction. In his poem "In Memoriam A.H.H.," Alfred, Lord Tennyson, wrote: "'Tis better to have loved and lost, / Than never to have loved at all." Those suffering from omission bias would disagree.

Omission bias in the workplace is why we will put up with poor performance from some individuals instead of replacing them with someone else who might do a better job. We'd rather do nothing than potentially hire another poorly performing employee. It's why we'd rather stick with the suboptimal process than try and fix it but end up with another suboptimal process. It's why we as workers might put up with poor working conditions instead of finding something better—because the new gig might be just as bad, we fear, and then we'd be in a bad situation by our own doing.

Embracing or encouraging a "test and learn" mindset is a good way to try and overcome omission bias. Said differently, it needs to be okay to fail. Failure needs to be viewed not as something to be avoided at all costs, but instead as a necessary step toward ultimate success. Henry Ford once said, "There is no disgrace in honest failure; there is disgrace in fearing to fail."[7] Organizations that embrace such a philosophy are far less likely to exhibit omission bias.

We've just learned that because of the status quo bias, we will sometimes unconsciously choose to remain in a suboptimal state, even though there may be better options available to us. Status quo bias keeps us in our current state, even if that means missing out on potential benefits. I want to take a short break from thinking about our colleagues' predisposition to change, and I want us to now turn inward for a moment, toward ourselves.

▸ Have you ever found yourself in a rut, perhaps feeling unable to get yourself out of the current state?

▸ Do you ever feel like you've been doing the same thing so long that you might be bored?

---

7 Ford, Henry and Crowther, Samuel. *My Life and Work*. Garden City, NY: Garden City Publishing Co., Inc., 1922.

▸ Do you ever start a new year wanting to make inspiring resolutions, but you aren't sure where to start or what to do?

▸ Does the mountain ahead sometimes seem too tall to climb or too wide to go around, so instead you stay right where you are?

This, my friend, is because you're suffering from the status quo bias. You're sticking with the current state, even if that means missing out on potential benefits. And do you know why you're doing that? It's not because you're lazy, or undedicated, or unmotivated, or flawed. You're there because you are human. And because you possess a human brain. So first, I want you to give yourself a break and respect your greatness. Now, let's talk about how to get yourself out of that rut. To do that, I'll tell you a story of my own status quo bias and how I pulled myself out of it.

LEARNING TO STRETCH

January 2015. I had been doing well at work, but I was a little bit bored. So I gave some serious thought to what skills I needed to work on, to just improve myself in some way. I needed to stretch. I needed to grow. And the thing that kept showing itself in my particular situation and in my particular industry was public speaking.

Ah, public speaking. It made me break a sweat just thinking about it. You know how when you're at the doctor's office, the moment before the nurse puts on the blood pressure cuff, well, that's the moment that your blood pressure skyrockets? Ah, that's exactly how I felt just thinking about public speaking. I think I had known for a couple years that I should be doing more public speaking in my profession, but I was just so darned scared. I remember one time years earlier, I was in a big meeting and by mistake I said "fucker" instead of "factor." I was horrified. After that incident, whenever I pictured myself on stage in front of a large crowd, I fully expected myself to be talking about lots of varied and important fuckers.

I had recently learned about these decision biases that we fall into simply because we're human. And so I gave myself a bit of grace. I wasn't flawed—I was just human. And I recognized that I was stuck in the status quo bias. Specifically, I was operating under the omission bias. Doing nothing and not progressing seemed unconsciously preferable to attempting public speaking and being an absolute disaster. But once I learned what was happening in my human brain, only then did I feel capable of actually changing it.

I decided that during 2015 I was going to sign up for as many public speaking opportunities as I could, hoping that by year end, I could easily conquer them without fear. I started with a simple Lunch and Learn at work. I trained a group of actuaries on predictive analytics and big data. Admittedly these actuaries all reported to me, but I needed to take baby steps, people!

I was in graduate school at the time, so I also presented to my classmates on group projects. I signed up for some local actuarial meetings. And later, some larger industry meetings. I presented on topics I knew well. I learned that everything sounds better if you practice. Keep practicing! My hour-plus commute was now spent reciting slides. The more I talked them out, the more natural sounding they became. I selected presentation outfits that wouldn't distract me—heels that were easy to walk in, blouses that didn't come untucked when I raised my arms, skirts with pockets or belts to hold microphone packs. I'd arrive on locations with enough time to practice once more before the main event. I learned to memorize word for word the entire first paragraph, because it was still taking me a few minutes to settle myself down as I spoke, and I needed to be able to deliver the first bit without thinking. I learned to always find a friendly audience member in the crowd—that one person who was smiling and engaged and simply happy to be there. Then, when I needed a bit of reassurance, I'd just look out at my new "friend."

In October of 2015, just ten months into this mini-adventure, I presented a session at a large conference to about four hundred listeners. I had developed a mini-following by that point. It was standing room only. I remember learning later that out of 189 sessions in the conference, attendees rated mine number two.

Things began to snowball for me after that. I began receiving invitations to speak domestically and internationally. I was offered opportunities to guest lecture at universities and present keynotes at various events. National Geographic asked me to film a short bit for a documentary series called *Breakthrough*. I was the featured speaker at the largest university TEDx event in the US.

What's interesting is that through all of this, I never actually kicked my fear of public speaking. I have presented to tens of thousands of people, and I still get scared. But I've learned that I can do it anyway. Despite my fear, I've pulled myself out of my rut, learned

Surviving and Thriving: Living Beyond a Distracted Life. At the Annenberg Center for the Performing Arts, Philadelphia, PA. Image courtesy of Ellen Bates.

to stretch, embraced many rich experiences, and helped thousands of people. As many people before me have shared, bravery is not the absence of fear. It's taking action despite fear. You, too, are brave. You, too, can push forward toward more. So the next time you have a little bit of quiet time—perhaps your commute, or your shower, or when you lay your head down to sleep at the end of your long day— give some thought as to whether you may be stuck in the status quo. And if you are, recognize that it is because you are human. And then, perhaps, think of a few tiny baby steps that you can take to push yourself out of whatever rut you may be in. In fact, reading this book, and learning to build your own winning conditions, is a step in itself. You can do this, and I am excited for you!

Anyway . . . before my personal digression, we learned that if all signs indicate action, and your colleague is tending toward inaction, then perhaps they're suffering from a status quo bias. But, what if their brain is rationally choosing inaction and instead it is YOUR brain that is irrationally suggesting change? Are there decision biases that influence action when, in fact, inaction might be the better choice? Can biases affect the skydivers on the other side of the adoption curve? Why, yes. Let's head back in time to a century or so ago, just to mix things up a little bit, and because this is a great example of an action bias that we've all heard about.

ACTION BIASES

In April 1912, the luxury ocean liner *Titanic* set out on her maiden voyage, carrying some twenty-two hundred passengers and crew. She was by all accounts one of the largest, fastest, and most magnificent ships ever built. She boasted state-of-the-art technology. Her extravagant design spared no expense for the über-wealthy passengers aboard, including a swimming pool, four elevators, and a first-class dining room. (The immigrants were packed below into steerage.) The *Titanic*'s hull was cleverly designed to render the ship unsinkable—four of her sixteen compartments could completely flood and yet the *Titanic* would still remain afloat. A leading-edge communication system and a modern electrical control panel contributed to her forward-thinking innovation. Clearly, the *Titanic* was the best of her kind. Anyone would be foolish to think otherwise.

Yet just four days into her journey, on the evening of April 14, 1912, she struck an iceberg, and just two and a half hours later, in the early-morning hours of April 15, she descended into the icy waters of the Atlantic Ocean. More than fifteen hundred passengers and crew perished that night, when the "unsinkable" *Titanic* sank. The deaths were blamed on an insufficient number of lifeboats and insufficient training. The ship was traveling too fast, and a key iceberg warning was dismissed. Poor weather conditions may have prevented the lookouts—who had no binoculars—from seeing the iceberg clearly.

Many suggest that these failures were a result of *action-oriented biases*—which are the opposite of *status quo biases*. Action-oriented biases relate to our propensity to act without sufficient accurate information and analysis. Action-oriented biases drive us to take action less thoughtfully than we should. We may drive forward without the appropriate checks, insurances, reinforcements, validations, or warranties. We feel pressure to take action, and we don't consider all of the potential ramifications. This is skydiving before you've double-checked your parachute. It's releasing an app before you've implemented thorough cybersecurity precautions. It's sending a company-wide email without spell-checking.

Action-oriented biases include:

Overconfidence—We may believe that our judgment is more accurate than another person's judgment. We overstate the accuracy of our own judgment. Those of us suffering from overconfidence might think that we are better than others, or that our product or service is necessarily better, not because it actually is better, but because we are irrationally overconfident. To understand overconfidence, we need only consider our opinions on our personal driving habits. Consider your own. Do you think your driving skills are better than average, or worse than average? If you're like 93 percent of American drivers,[8] you think you drive better than the average driver. By definition of the word *average*, only 50 percent can drive better than average. So how do we get to 93 percent? Overconfidence.

The *Titanic*'s skipper, Captain E. J. Smith, was (over)confident in his ability to judge the appropriate speed given the weather and ocean conditions. Consequently, he was going too fast. The radio operator Jack Phillips was (over)confident in his ability to recognize the urgency and seriousness of messages. Consequently, he neglected to pass along a message from the ship *Californian*, which relayed critical information about the dense ice field ahead.

We see this in the present-day workplace as well. Sometimes people become so entrenched in their own work and their own solutions that they believe them to work for every situation. They believe their judgment is better than everyone else's. My data trumps your dumb anecdotes. My claims processing product is right for you, regardless of whether you're currently satisfied or dissatisfied. My solutions are appropriate, and I don't care what you've tried in the past and whether that's worked for you or not.

It's sometimes tricky to diagnose our own overconfidence, because there can be a fuzzy line between what we know and what we think we know. Have you stopped asking questions because you think you already know the answers? Do you consistently tune out other people's opinions because they aren't as experienced as you are? Do you always prefer your own solutions in every situation? Do your colleagues repeatedly ask you for additional information, backup, or documentation before they will support your work? Any of these might be clues that you may be exhibiting some overconfidence.

An overabundance of confidence can be harmful. When you

---

8 Svenson, Ola. "Are We All Less Risky and More Skillful Than Our Fellow Drivers?" *Acta Psychologica* 47 (1981): 143–148.

judge yourself or your product in an irrationally too-positive way, your business partners might question your judgment and, therefore, also question your suggestion to act. So before you tout the superiority, dominance, or absolute advantages of your work or ideas, give some serious thought as to whether those claims are realistic or potentially the result of your human brain's overconfidence.

Excessive optimism—We may believe we are less likely than others to experience a negative event. Those of us with optimism bias focus on only part of the issue—the positive part that we want to see. Then, we may take on too much risk, or act before ensuring the right insurances or conditions are in place for our ideas to realistically succeed.

Due to excessive optimism, the *Titanic*'s builders outfitted the ship with only about half of the recommended lifeboats. After all, there was no need to clutter the decks of an unsinkable ship. Training was insufficient because, well, she won't sink! The key to the ship's store of binoculars was inadvertently left behind when the *Titanic* set out, but the excessive optimism of all aboard this magnificent ship masked the possibility of disaster. So no one, including the lookouts, ever bothered to secure binoculars at all.

Excessive optimism is why some people experience financial ruin by being uninsured or underinsured. They may not expect to face a serious illness. They may not expect their homes to be damaged by fire or earthquake or hurricane or flood. They may not expect the worst of life's adverse events, which sadly do happen to some. It is excessive optimism when you think, "Oh, but that won't happen to me." The 2008 financial crisis may have been the worst economic disaster since the Great Depression—many believe it occurred because of excessive optimism.

Just like you did with overconfidence, before you sell your work or idea or product or service, make sure that you have considered both the potential advantages and disadvantages associated with it.

Consider the downstream positive and negative outcomes. Consider the potential positive and negative influences.

Overall, to best mitigate potential action-oriented biases, balance is the key. You may rightfully have the best product or the best idea. You'll just want to be sure that you have completed all of the proper analysis, review, and exploration before automatically touting your product or service as superior to all others. It's checking your parachute one last time before you jump.

Our discussion thus far about winning conditions has centered on the people that are involved in and impacted by the delivery of your work. We've explored the concepts around best understanding motivations and situations. We've learned how to manage messaging based on the details that matter. We've talked about awareness of potential biases that might impact our decisions.

Now I want to move away from specific business interactions or engagements and move into personal ways that we can actually create more opportunities for success. I want to consider strategies for *being* and *behaving* in the workplace that can help build winning conditions.

We'll start by creating experiences in Chapter 8.

PART 3:

ELEVATE YOURSELF

CHAPTER 8

CREATE
EXPERIENCES

submitted my first *Survivor* application in the summer of 2001. It was a multipage questionnaire I filled out by hand and a three-minute video that was recorded onto a big, fat VHS tape. In the video, I was running through my back woods in a tank top and shorts, finding and solving clues I had preplanted. In one scene my little boys were nestled under a tree. My Andrew was two years old, my baby, Mike, just six months. I mailed the application in a standard nine-by-twelve-inch manila envelope through the US Postal Service. I wasn't selected. But I wasn't giving up on my dream.

I submitted my second *Survivor* application in the summer of 2002. Same handwritten answers, same big, fat VHS tape, same snail-mail delivery. Except this time, I answered the front door wearing only Saran Wrap, telling the viewer, "I heard you can't say no to a woman wearing Saran Wrap." My mom filmed that video! They indeed said no. But I wasn't giving up on my dream.

By the summer of 2016, I was still submitting applications. By now my babies were teenagers, and now there were three—Andrew and Mike had been joined by their sister, Elise. These three alternately filmed and edited my videos, which were decidedly less risqué and involved no Saran Wrap. Alternating between the kids had allowed me to continue applying to play The Game more frequently than any one person in my family knew. Over the years, the questionnaire became decidedly shorter, and it was now electronic instead of handwritten. The video was still three minutes, but those big, fat VHS tapes didn't even exist anymore. Now, videos were filmed on a smartphone and uploaded directly to the internet.

And finally, after all those years, I got the call I'd been waiting for.

In the spring of 2017, I finally lived my dream of competing on the greatest reality television show of all time. And people now tell me that "I'm so lucky" I got to play. Most of them want to play also. They wish they could play. They dream of playing. Oh, to have a chance to play! But when I ask how often they've applied, the answer is generally consistent—never.

There's a sixteenth-century proverb that tells us "Diligence is the mother of good luck," and I believe it—people we consider "lucky" actually work quite diligently to secure their success. They engage with others frequently. They seek out experiences and interactions again and again. They don't view a failure as a failure but, instead, as a step closer to success. They actively create positive experiences by pushing forward and relating with as many people as possible. Let me say that again with emphasis:

Successful people actively create positive experiences by pushing forward and relating with as many people as possible.

When you continue to create interactions for yourself, then eventually one or more of these experiences will return to provide some positive lift. Is that luck? Or simply effort? It is certainly winning conditions.

You've learned that winning conditions means being consciously aware of new perspectives and looking outward to address the needs of others. Now it's time to turn inward and look at the personal steps we can take to increase our opportunities for success. In this chapter, we'll explore the idea of frequent interactions and experiences, and how increasing the number of interactions that you have in (and out of) the workplace can increase your likelihood of success. In subsequent chapters we'll talk about how to increase the value of each individual interaction to further boost your wins.

PERSISTENCY

Creating frequent interactions—being persistent—breeds success in two ways. The first and probably more obvious has to do with probabilities. This is how I landed a spot on *Survivor*. I'll explain it using an urn full of marbles.

Pretend that you have an urn containing one white marble for everything you do in a given day, week, or month that *does not* advance your own personal hopes or dreams. Such activities could include going to the grocery store, driving the carpool, feeding the family pet, paying bills, clearing spam email out of your in-box, or anything-you-agreed-to-do-even-though-you-wish-you'd-said-no-because-you-don't-really-have-time-for-it-and-don't-want-to-do-it-anyway.

Pretend that you have a red marble in that urn for everything you do in a given day, week, or month that you feel *does* move you closer to achieving your goals. Such activities could include positive engagements with colleagues, listening to a podcast, connecting with someone on LinkedIn, volunteering, meeting a new person, writing an article, taking a class, or filming an audition video for a reality television game you really want to play.

Now, if you generally keep to yourself without engaging others or aren't working to make positive forward strides toward your own goals, then you'll be left carrying an urn full of white marbles. This is what happens when we fall into a rut of just going through the motions. This is what happens when we don't extend ourselves. This is what happens when we always put other people's needs before our own. I'll ask you to reach into your urn full of only white marbles and, without looking, please draw out a red marble. If you draw red, you win.

Obviously, without any red marbles in the urn—with zero engagements or interactions or forward strides toward your own goals—your likelihood of achieving those goals is zero. Walking around with an urn full of white marbles can be super discouraging. If we never do anything to advance our goals, we'll never reach our goals. We deserve more. But sometimes we just get caught up in the daily grind. Sometimes it's hard to reach out and engage.

If you never get yourself out there, your likelihood of winning is zero.

Wayne Gretzky is rumored to have quipped in a 1983 interview with Bob McKenzie, "You miss 100 percent of the shots you never take."[9] So true. Let's fix that together.

Let's take that shot. Maybe you will create a new experience, say hello to a colleague you've never met, or reach out to that recruiter to get some more information on that position you've been eyeing. For this one interaction, I'll place one red marble into the urn full of white marbles, mix them up, and again ask you to reach in without looking. If you draw out a red marble, you win. Now there is some likelihood of winning, although it's small.

So let's take a second shot. This time when you engage, perhaps you write a post on LinkedIn, tweet, publish a blog post, or send a letter of thanks to a colleague who introduced you to a new opportunity. I'll place a second red marble into the urn. The urn now contains two red marbles and many white marbles. Without looking,

---

9   Burnside, S., Custance, C., Goldstein, S., Grant, P., Kavanagh, T., LeBrun, P., and McDonald, J. "55 Shades of Great: Random facts about Wayne Gretzky on his 55th birthday," ESPN.com, January 21, 2016, https://www.espn.com/nhl/story/_/id/14621635/nhl-55-shades-great-facts-wayne-gretzky-55th-birthday

can you select red? Continue engaging, creating experiences, and adding red marbles one by one and repeating the experiment.

It's easy to see that the more red marbles we place into the urn, the more likely we are to draw red and win. The more engagements and forward momentum toward our goals that we can create, the more likely we are to achieve a winning outcome. Is this luck? No, it's math. When you persist, you create more opportunity for success, and so your likelihood of success is greater. When you continue to create interactions, then eventually one or more of these experiences or contacts will return to provide some positive lift. My persistent *Survivor* applications were simply providing more opportunities for me to be noticed and selected.

Why not think about each positive interaction that you have with your colleagues as a red marble in that urn? Each time you engage with someone else, you give yourself another chance at a win. You move closer to some positive outcome. You may not see the result immediately, but you will see it eventually. Because with each interaction, you are creating another opportunity to build trust. You are generating another opportunity for a yes. You are practicing and perfecting your approach.

Fund-raisers suggest it takes an average of three asks to secure a donation. Old-school marketing rules suggest it takes an average of seven impressions for your product to even register consciously with a customer. As I write this book my son Andrew (now a college student) is applying for summer internships. I recently suggested to him that if he submits ten applications, he might be lucky to hear back from one firm. So he may want to consider submitting twenty applications. Or thirty. When he finally gets that internship, it won't be from luck, but instead, persistence.

Each time you engage, you put another red marble into the urn. How often do you actually interact *in person* with your colleagues? If you have an opportunity to be physically present at a work event or meeting, then be physically present. Actively work to create those engagements. I've worked in offices where the meeting is down the hall but people don't actually attend it in person. Instead, they will dial in from their cubicles or offices. Please don't do this! I know it's work, and sometimes it's uncomfortable—trust me, I'm an introvert (more on this later). But you need to get out and create experiences so that you can create opportunities. When you're physically at the table, engaged and listening, then others can see you're part of the decisions. They will value your contributions. These engagements could lead to additional opportunities, so be visible!

It's not always possible to attend events in person, though. Present-day technology has enabled the expansion of the remote worker, which complicates the ability to have in-person contact. If you work remotely, do you have any opportunities to travel to the office of your organization or customer? Are you able to use webcam technology like FaceTime or Skype to create virtual in-person meetings when travel is not possible or too costly? If telephone is your only option, then be mindful of creating an optimal professional phone presence. Ensure that you have a good connection without interference. Minimize or eliminate background noise, such as barking dogs, a blaring television, or other unexpected distractions. Stay engaged throughout the call and add value to the conversation as appropriate. Don't use that conference call as an opportunity to multitask, answer emails, or beat the daily challenge on your Solitaire app. Convey professionalism, energy, and enthusiasm with your vocal tones. If you actually smile while you're on the phone, then you'll be more likely to convey a positive tone. Speak clearly and with purpose. This phone interaction is a contact point— be "visible"!

Consider varying your approach—how many *different ways* and to how many *different people* can you make your presence known? There are so many ways that you can create interactions in the workplace. Attend the quarterly town hall or financial update meeting in person instead of by phone. Sit at a table with people you've never met. Bring business cards if you have them, and make new connections. (Remember to add your new connections later to LinkedIn, too!) Join the company gym—it will not only improve your health but will also improve your visibility. With each visit, you're adding red marbles to your jar. Be visible!

Eat lunch in the cafeteria (even if you've brought your lunch from home). Sign up to present something you know at the next team meeting. Organize a charity event. Join a workplace special interest group. Train the new hire. Volunteer to serve ice cream for an hour at the company picnic. If you're a manager, you can raise your visibility by participating in the practice of "management by wandering around," a phrase that actually became an acronym— MBWA. MBWA suggests that managers can successfully run their teams by walking around in an unstructured manner, checking in periodically with team members at random. Besides getting status updates, the managers are *being seen*. Whether you're an individual contributor or a leader of people, think about ways that you can get yourself out there. Be visible!

These ideas for increased visibility may not work for you if your organization is small or if you're self-employed. In those cases, try to increase your visibility in your *industry* as a means of increasing engagement. Enroll in industry seminars. Bring your business cards, if you have them. Again, make new connections and later add these new connections on LinkedIn. Volunteer to speak at a conference. Share your knowledge. Work a booth. Write an article. Highlight your work, service, or product through the internet and social media channels. Post relevant updates on LinkedIn, Twitter, Instagram, Facebook, or other sites. Email. Tweet. Write a blog. Whatever you can think of. There are so many examples, you just need to *get yourself out there*. Be visible!

When my son was applying for that internship, we gave some thought to how he could add to his presence and be more visible. The solution: besides submitting his résumé online, my son also checked his LinkedIn network to see if any of his existing contacts work at the firms to which he applied. Wherever he knew someone at the firm, he also emailed his résumé directly to his contact and asked them to submit it directly to the hiring manager and to the human resources team. The target companies would actually receive his résumé multiple times—once from his online submission and again from an internal contact. It's varied persistence.

We've all probably heard the quip "It's not *what* you know, it's *who* you know." In my experience, the more accurate quip is:

It's not who you know, it's WHO KNOWS YOU.

The more people that know you, know about you, and respect you and your work, the more likely you are to win. You need to get yourself out there and allow as many people as possible to know your value, know what you have to offer, know your experience, know that you are in demand. Every time someone interacts with YOU, it's one more red marble for you in that urn. I want you to remember that you are outstanding. You are exceptional. You are working hard, and you are striving to better yourself. You are motivated and dedicated. You take pride in your work and all that you have to offer. The more often you can get yourself out there, the more people will know how valuable you are.

What will YOU do? What opportunities can you take advantage of—this week, this month, this year—that will enable others to learn more about you? Think about how you can actively create positive experiences by pushing forward and engaging with people as often as possible.

But there's more.

THE MERE EXPOSURE EFFECT

I wrote earlier that "persistency breeds success in two ways." The first, as we learned, is based on simple math—when you increase the number of engagements, then eventually one or more of these interactions will return to provide some positive lift. The second is based on another phenomenon of our glorious human brains. (I bet you didn't expect to learn so much about your human brain!) That is, repeated experiences and interactions cause a sense of familiarity. That familiarity creates a feeling of acceptance. Acceptance influences preference. And we are more likely to say yes to the people and things that we prefer.

Repeated experience → Familiarity → Acceptance → Preference = "YES!"

This whole process is the called the *mere exposure effect* (often shortened for brevity to the *exposure effect*), and was developed by social psychologist Robert Zajonc in the 1960s. Basically, the more often you are exposed to something, the more your brain likes it and the more likely you are to say yes to it. Said differently, mere exposure leads to a more positive impression and a greater likelihood of acceptance.

When I was a stay-at-home mom, I worked a few hours a week at the local J.Crew. Whenever the new collections were rolled out, we'd get a huge shipment of the new pieces, and a group of us would pull an all-nighter while we packed away the old clothes and steamed, hung, folded, and displayed the new clothes. It was actually a lot of fun. I was a mom of three kids and at least a decade or two older than my younger, cooler, single colleagues. Despite the difference in age and life circumstance, I adored them—except when they blasted hip-hop music. All night. On full volume. I thought my eardrums would bleed—I didn't like the music choices at all. But what's interesting is that after a few rollouts, I started to recognize the songs. Oh yeah! This is the boots-with-the-fur one! That club can't handle me! (I know I'm a dork—just go with it.) I actually started to get to know the words—AND I STARTED LIKING IT. To this day, I love to listen to hip-hop. I may or may not be able to rap entire Eminem songs . . . Anyway, this is classic exposure effect.

It's the same way with people. If others are exposed to you more frequently, then you will become familiar to them. They will begin to accept you. They will be more likely to say yes to you and your work.

Let's look again at the internship example. The first time a résumé is received from an online portal, it is a stranger's résumé. But when it's again received from an internal contact, now it's no longer a stranger. Now . . . oh, I remember this one! I've seen this one before! Now it's familiar. Familiarity means this résumé is now liked a little bit more than it was on the first view. It's also liked a little more than all the other applications from the online portal that have only been viewed once. Therefore, it's more likely to be accepted for next steps. (Note: I recognize that this example disregards the positive effects of a personal recommendation, which would support the win even beyond the exposure effect. Nonetheless, the additional views leading to a sense of familiarity will increase the affinity and preference.)

When you attend the town hall in person and sit at a table with colleagues you've never met, your colleagues have seen you once. If you happen to bump into them again at an internal meeting, now you're familiar. And because they have human brains, they actually like you more than they would if you were a total stranger. Familiarity may lead to your contributions at this internal meeting being more highly accepted. This could lead to a win.

Repeat for all the other times you've created an interaction—in the cafeteria, at the charity event, at the company picnic. Assuming you weren't highly offensive or otherwise acting inappropriately, you've leveraged the exposure effect to your benefit. This is why it's recommended to add a professional photo to your LinkedIn profile—when people see your online post, they recognize you by sight. Then you become familiar, accepted, and preferred. This is why going to the company gym, joining a special interest group, or engaging on Twitter may be counted as red marbles—because these also advance your likelihood of a win.

You can also use the exposure effect for your projects. Consider everyone who will be a part of your project life cycle at some point. Reach out to each of them now. Introduce your project early. Even if you have cross-functional business partners you won't "need" for a few weeks or months, check in with them sooner. Let them know that you'll be seeking their approval or feedback on this project later. Tell them all about your project. Tell them you're looking forward to incorporating their valuable expertise into the project's outcome or solution. Make sure that your colleagues recognize that they are a valuable part of your project's success. The purposeful contact early (rather than at the absolute last moment, when you finally need them) will encourage familiarity, and the familiarity will encourage acceptance. When it comes time to actually work together on that project, your colleagues will already feel comfortable with it. You will have boosted your likelihood of success.

THE STALKER

But when does repeated exposure simply become annoying?

Years ago, I was working at a large organization where I was contacted by someone who was conducting research on diversity within the industry for a magazine article they were writing. They politely asked for thirty minutes of my time to gather information on my organization's hiring practices and diversity efforts. Our chief diversity officer (CDO) also joined the call to share her expertise. We were happy to help, and the short time commitment was manageable.

During the thirty-minute call, we got through only about half of the questions. CDO and I asked the researcher to email us the remaining questions so that we could provide written responses. After submitting the written responses, they asked for thirty more minutes by phone to review. We were coming up on a crazy year end and had already devoted a chunk of time to this effort, but we nonetheless agreed. But thirty more minutes wasn't enough for them. They proceeded to call and email repeatedly day after day to keep asking more and more questions and ask for more and more time. And it didn't stop.

Their polite became pushy. Their ask became interrogation. Every interaction became more and more uncomfortable. They wouldn't stop calling. They wouldn't stop emailing. They reached out multiple times a day. CDO and I eventually needed to shut down the whole situation completely. We were alarmed that this could escalate further. We ultimately stayed as far away from that researcher as possible. We both think of that as a terrible experience. In this case, the researcher pushed past the breaking point. They put so many red marbles in the urn that the urn broke.

This is what happens when people grow tired of persistence. This is what happens when the radio jingle becomes an earworm, when the frequent emails turn into flooding an in-box, when checking up becomes stalking. This is what happens when you persist to the breaking point. Don't persist to the breaking point. The breaking point is losing conditions.

But how do you know what the breaking point is? Well, there's no one-size-fits-all answer for that. The breaking point will be different depending on the application and the people involved. You'll need to put on your conscious-awareness hat. Are you beginning to notice a change in the level of warmth or engagement in your interactions? Is your audience taking longer and longer to reply to your outreach, or have they mentioned more than a few times that they're too busy to work with you on something? Do they seem uninterested, or have they stopped responding altogether? While some of these examples might be the result of an entirely unrelated event (your colleague might truly be busy with another project, or bad-tempered because of another experience), becoming aware can help you avoid hitting the breaking point in your own interactions. Ultimately your goal is to create positive experience without creating overload.

CHRISTINE HOFBECK

PUTTING YOURSELF OUT THERE

Before we close out this idea of creating experiences, let's consider a few other things. First, as you're upping your engagements, be mindful of knowing your audience so that you can set realistic expectations of potential results. Marketing teams often rely on something called a *hit rate* to measure the success of their sales efforts. The hit rate is the number of successful sales divided by the number of sales attempts. So if you want to increase the number of successful sales (wins), you probably want to increase the number of attempts. But not always. Potential customers must have some likelihood of purchasing the product in order for this relationship to work. For example, marketing butter to vegans will result in a low likelihood of sale whether you market your butter to ten vegans or ten thousand vegans (because vegans don't consume animal products). If my son applies to twenty executive-level openings, he hasn't increased his likelihood of securing an internship, because he's unqualified for an executive role given his current level of experience. So be aware of relevancy of engagement as you are selecting the red marbles to add to your urn.

Does this mean you should completely avoid experiences that have little relevance to your current or future work? Absolutely not. Rich experiences add to the interest that is our lives. Even experiences without a direct and visible connection to our current roles will serve to improve our diversity of thought and understanding. They improve our confidence. They provide additional practice opportunities for positive engagement, as well as educational opportunities. They give us great stories. Experiences make us who we are.

Survivor was totally unrelated to my career but ended up being a huge boost to my professional success, because it boosted my relevance and recognition. It enhanced the exposure effect. At some point I'd like to spend six months working at McMurdo research station in Antarctica. If I were lucky enough to be selected for that, then it would most definitely be a red marble, even though my work would be completely unrelated to the actuarial field. I'd probably be working as a cashier at the grocery or in food prep in the kitchen, not building actuarial models and managing clients. But that doesn't matter to me. It's the stuff of life. So give some thought as to how you can create positive experiences and generate engagements as often as possible. Enrich your life. Learn. Live. Create. Meet people. Be extraordinary.

Do this even when it seems impossible to find the time . . . which is the next thing I want us to consider. The truth is, most of us have about five hundred things already on our plates. We're caring for our kids, caring for our families, caring for our friends, caring for our homes, caring for others in our communities. How do we even find an extra moment in there to care for OURSELVES? I hear you. I really do. When it seems impossible to find the time, take a deep breath and give yourself some grace. Then remember what every flight attendant since the beginning of time has advised:

> *"In the event of a sudden drop in cabin pressure, oxygen masks will drop from the ceiling. Please secure your own mask before helping others."*

Securing your own mask means maybe you can fit in one extra little thing to help write YOUR winning story. That's one more marble, and you should be proud of that. Then maybe you can fit in one more little thing later. This doesn't need to be all or nothing. Every red marble increases your opportunity. So if right now you can manage two, then those are two excellent marbles. If you can find a way to add a third, then great. If you can't, that's okay. Two is better than zero. Just do what you can. Every marble counts.

There's a common expression that if you want to do something, you'll make time; if you don't want to do something, you'll make excuses. I try to thoughtfully consider what I really want to do, and then do that. Those are my red marbles. Things that I don't really want to do dilute my ability to add reds. So I make excuses for these things, and then I forgive myself for making those excuses. Right now I have a lot of *Survivor* fans asking me for birthday video shout-outs and audition tape feedback. I just can't right now, and I let that be okay. I get at least five LinkedIn messages a week from strangers asking me for short phone calls on things that seem outside my scope of expertise or interest. I just can't right now, and I let that be okay. Friends ask me if I'll just talk for a few minutes to their neighbor's nephew's roommate's brother about becoming an actuary. I just can't right now, and I let that be okay. Even though each of these asks only takes a few minutes, those minutes add up. Instead, I'm extending myself in other ways that are meaningful to me.

Think about your life—what are your red marbles? How can you add more of them to the urn?

Lastly, I want to acknowledge that creating repetitive and positive engagements with others can be more difficult for those of you (us) who are introverts. Yes, I wrote earlier in this chapter that I'm an introvert. Just to be clear, the definition of an introvert is someone who restores their energy by being alone. In contrast, an extrovert is someone who gains energy by being with people. So creating experiences can at times be draining, not exhilarating, for introverts.

Creating experiences can also be scary for people who are shy—or even people who aren't. Remember me and public speaking? That was terrifying to me, but I managed to do it anyway. Here's another one—beginning my graduate program. I remember so clearly the morning of my first day. I woke up, pulled off the covers, put my feet on the floor, paused for a moment . . . and then I just put my head in my hands in panic. I was convinced that I was going to be a total disaster. I thought that everyone else would be so much smarter than me, and I'd feel so out of place, and the whole experience would be infinitely embarrassing and humiliating. I didn't think I could do it. But I made myself do it. I put one foot in front of the other and packed my bag and got on the plane and did it. And you know what? It was wonderful, one of the best experiences of my entire life.

And that's the point. "Draining" or "scary" does not mean "impossible." It's definitely work for me to walk into a room of people I've never met and pretend I'm comfortable. It's definitely work for me to stand up in front of a room of people to give a presentation. It's definitely work for me to engage on social media—even something as simple as posting or tweeting or sharing an article. But I do it anyway, whenever I can, because each of these is a red marble. Each of these is winning conditions.

You can do it, too. Whatever is out there that you want to do but that scares you—do it anyway. You can. You will. I'll be cheering for you. You are going be great. I know it's work. I know it's hard. But it's not impossible. Take a deep breath and go for it anyway. Each step we take toward creating experiences brings us one step closer to our own winning stories.

Putting ourselves out there (without stalking!) can lead to a rich diversity of experiences and lots of future wins. Consider your visibility in the workplace, in your industry, and in your life experiences. Let other people meet you and know you. Accept that invitation, get out of your chair, make that call, and enjoy that experience. You have so much to offer the world. Remember, it's not who you know, it's who knows you. You are a gift.

And then just wait for all your friends and family to tell you how lucky you've become!

So we've just talked about the importance of the *quantity* of interactions. But increasing the number of red marbles isn't the only way to build winning conditions. What if you could also increase the size of the red marbles relative to the white? You can! In the next few chapters, we'll explore how to increase the *quality* of each of your individual interactions. Read on!

CHAPTER 9

DEFINE YOUR
OWN VALUE

I n the early 2010s, I was living in New Jersey and working in downtown Manhattan. Remember that four-hour round-trip commute? Yes—those were the days. I used to wake up before 5 a.m. so I could leave my house by 5:45 a.m. latest. Anything past that, and traffic would stall me on Route 78 for far too long. Even with no traffic, I faced a ninety-minute drive to the Jersey City parking lot. I'd park my old clunker on the New Jersey side of the Hudson River, buy a ticket, and take the New York Waterway ferry across the river. After a short ferry ride, I'd disembark near the South Street Seaport and dash a few blocks to my office building on Maiden Lane. I was always eager to just make it to my desk by that point. Two hours since I left my house, and I was ready to "start" my day.

I worked on the twenty-seventh floor, and so each morning, despite my hurry, I still needed to pause for a few minutes to wait for the elevator. Every once in a blue moon, I'd turn into the elevator bank and there would be an open elevator just waiting for me. Those days started off right! I remember one morning I saw an elevator on the ground floor, its doors in the process of closing, and I very unprofessionally (but I thought quite skillfully) launched myself and my four-inch heels directly into that elevator. No, sir, I was not waiting for the next one! Imagine my surprise and embarrassment when I saw there was already a well-dressed gentleman inside. He chuckled a little bit at me, my face turned beet red, but then we both settled into typical elevator behavior: "Look straight ahead, say nothing." A minute later, I was released from my embarrassment when the doors opened and I bailed out onto twenty-seven. My typical day ensued, and ten or so hours later I was managing the reverse commute back home.

Next morning, a similar routine. Up, out, drive, park, ticket, ferry, dash, elevators. And for the second day in a row—I am a lucky girl!—elevator on the ground floor. Heck, those doors are half closing again, but I know I can make it! Launch! Success.

I think I heard the chuckle before I saw the man. You guessed it. The well-dressed man, for the second day in a row, inside my elevator. This time, we broke convention. He asked me what I did on the twenty-seventh floor. So I reached out my hand to shake, and with a smile, announced, "Hi, I'm Christine. I'm an actuary." I thought I was so cool. Until he replied, "Hi, I'm David Herzog. I'm the CFO." And the moment he uttered those words, I knew I had just missed one great opportunity. Here's why—

In the last chapter, we learned that the *quantity* (or number) of interactions you have can positively correlate with your success— as one increases, the other does, too. This happens because both persistence and mere exposure breed success. But we should also be thinking about the *quality* (or value) of each individual interaction. That is, whenever we engage, are those interactions positively contributing to our success? Or are they just okay? The elevator story I shared above is a great example of how I absolutely did NOT maximize the quality of one important interaction. The CFO (chief financial officer—one of our highest-level executives) of a massive insurance company was essentially held captive to me for our short elevator ride. I shared my first name and my profession. I never shared my full name or my value. I only succeeded in making myself completely indistinguishable from everyone else. Or distinguishable only as "that crazy lady who launches herself unprofessionally into elevators every morning."

In the next two chapters, we'll explore ways that you can maximize the *quality* of your individual contact points. In this chapter, we'll cover how to best communicate and share your great value, and in Chapter 10 we'll talk about creating a sense of magnetism that inspires others to *want* to work with you.

RETRAINING THE AUTOPILOT

In our lives, we come across new and different people constantly—in the workplace, in the cafeteria, on the sidelines of our kids' soccer games, in the mall, in line at the local coffee shop, on the airplane, at the gym. Many of these interactions are brief, and we generally expect them to be uneventful, leaving little or no impact on our lives. Why? Probably because we don't have the brain space to be constantly alert to opportunity. It's exhausting. Many of us are juggling so many other responsibilities besides work—raising children, taking classes, caring for elderly parents, taking care of our homes and everything in them, volunteering, supporting community events, being a "good" spouse/partner/parent/friend/neighbor—that when asked what we do, we give an autopilot answer. Remember we talked about all the things we do mindlessly, like eating ice cream? Here's another one—responding to a stranger's query about what we do.

What do you do?

I'm in marketing.
I'm in real estate.
Human resources.
Management.
Creative design.
Sales.

When people ask us what we do, it's easier to simplify. We dumb it down. We give a one- or two-word answer. We make ourselves one-dimensional. We provide our role or department but forget to share the great value that we bring to that role or department. And while that may be acceptable for the stranger in the seat next to you on the airplane (especially when you have some time-critical work to catch up on, so you don't really have time to launch into a full discussion), we become accustomed to this simplified response. We automatically and robotically provide it to everyone—including the colleagues and industry contacts that we might meet at a workplace networking event.

So you've finally found just a little bit of time to attend that town hall! You sat down with people you've never met. Good for you! Or you ate lunch in your workplace cafeteria, or joined a workplace special interest group, or volunteered at the company picnic. Good for you! You are adding those red marbles to your jar! And your table mate or colleague asks:

What do you do?

I'm in marketing.
I'm in real estate.
Human resources.
Management.
Creative design.
Sales.

It's what I said to the gentleman in the elevator: "I'm an actuary." I shared my department. I did not share my individual and compelling value.

The problem here is that other people don't automatically know the great value that we bring to our work, our organizations, and our societies. We need to let them know. We need to advocate for ourselves. We need to speak up.

If you're still not sure, then think about any five people in your life. It could be your partner, your friend, your mom, your brother, your neighbor. Anyone. Now, think about their work, but more specifically, think about the unique and authentic value that they bring to their role. Do you even know what that differentiating value is? What makes these people outstanding at their roles? Or do you just know they're a manager, a designer, an author? "I'm an actuary."

Here's another thing to try. Ask those five people to tell you what *you* do. Do their replies showcase the greatness that is you? Do the replies showcase the incredibly positive and compelling qualities that you exhibit at work every day?

A few years ago I was working at a career fair at our local high school, and a student approached my table to ask me what an actuary does. I was thrilled that they were potentially interested in pursuing actuarial science. Alas, it turns out that was not the reason for their visit. Apparently their father was an actuary, but every time they asked their dad what he did, the dad replied simply, "I'm an actuary." The student had no idea what that meant, so they stopped asking him—and asked me instead.

WHAT IS AN ACTUARY?

Well, I can't write a whole chapter on explaining yourself and not share what an actuary does!

Briefly—an actuary uses patterns of historical data to predict the possible occurrence of future financial events (events that require one or more payments). How likely are the events to happen in the future? When might they happen? What would be the size of the payout?

We use this information to prudently plan (save) for those future payments, to mitigate financial risk, and to protect the well-being of people in our society.

Which brings up yet another problem of a one- or two-word response to the prompt "What do you do?" These types of replies tend to shut down a conversation, not cultivate one. They don't invite questions. Your audience may feel as if you're trying to end the conversation abruptly. Just like the student, they may not ask for more information. They may simply smile and walk away.

Winning conditions is making sure that our great value is understood, appreciated, and accepted. It means genuinely and accurately advocating for ourselves when engaging with our colleagues. It means opening up conversations that might lead to opportunities. With just a little practice, we can all learn how to do this—graciously and thoughtfully. Just like we can learn a better way to respond to praise, we can also retrain our autopilot responses to "What do you do?" We can learn to reflect the real versions of ourselves—the incredible, interesting, engaging, dynamic versions of ourselves that are adding value and differentiating us. We can do this without sounding egotistical and without embarking on a long and boring soliloquy. Whenever you're adding a red marble to your urn, you can make sure it's a LARGE red marble.

This is all much easier if you already have a great response ready to go, so let's work on that together.

THE ELEVATOR SPEECH

Have you ever heard of an *elevator speech*? An elevator speech is a short introduction that you provide during an initial encounter to express your value. Basically, when you first meet someone, instead of giving that one- or two-word automatic response that is really just your department, your role, or your profession, you instead share a couple of short, compelling sentences *that showcase your personal value* within that department, role, or profession. Despite its name, the initial encounter can happen anywhere—at the water cooler, at a conference, in the parking lot. I know that my encounter did actually happen in an elevator, but that was a freak accident.

An elevator speech actually gets its name from the idea that this short introduction takes about the same amount of time as an elevator ride—maybe twenty seconds or less. Ideally, when the figurative elevator doors open and the ride is done, the person with whom you're talking should be left wanting to hear more. Your goal is to provide just enough information that your audience understands, appreciates, and respects your value—without tuning you out.

Think about our imaginary friends who told us simply, "I'm in marketing" or "I'm in real estate."

What if instead of . . .	they tried . . .
I'm in marketing.	I find niches of the population that would be interested in buying my company's new line of housewares and then figure out how to get potential customers excited about the products. I'm focusing right now on incorporating Instagram influencers into our marketing, and so far that's been really effective.
I'm in real estate.	I'm a real estate agent in the Rockwell Township area. Actually, this past summer I sold those four homes over on Chestnut Street, which wasn't easy given the water issues in that area. But the buyers and sellers ended up thrilled in the end. My phone hasn't stopped ringing with referrals since!
Human resources.	I work on a program that makes sure that the managers in my organization always consider a diverse slate when they're hiring and promoting. Our company has been growing dramatically—and we know it's because of the enriched diversity of thought in our teams.
Management.	I manage a team of tech associates at the XYZ Company and all the projects and issues within the team. We're responsible for all the domestic technology updates for XYZ. Sometimes it's a juggling act, but I've cut turnover in half and feedback has been encouraging, so at least I'm creating some positive change!

Creative design.	I create the posters for ABC Supermarket chains that showcase the health benefits of produce. If you're interested in the fourteen nutritional advantages of arugula, or how kale reduces your risk of heart disease, let me know!
Sales.	I'm a salesperson at J.Crew. I have a lot of fun helping our customers look and feel great in the perfect outfit. And they get a big kick out of my love of math, because I always remember everyone's sizes. So the moment they enter the store, I can automatically pull the perfect pieces from the latest collections.

Do you see how each of these responses briefly showcases a unique value and enables the conversation to continue? *Ah, I'm intrigued! What are your new housewares? How do you find Instagram influencers? I was wondering who sold those homes on Chestnut! I heard those sales took only three days—incredible! Which homes are you representing now? That's fantastic that your company is growing so much. What do you do if there aren't diverse candidates in the pipeline? How did you cut turnover in half? What's arugula? How on earth are you able to remember all that?* You see, each of the more comprehensive—but brief—elevator responses enables the conversation to continue and allows value to be shared in an easy, conversational manner. (And yes, that last one was me.)

It's easy to see now why my opportunity with the CFO was wasted. "I'm an actuary," I said. I shared my profession, not my value. I shut down the conversation. The sad thing about this missed opportunity is that what I was doing in that actuarial role was actually quite innovative. I was building an entire predictive analytics capability for the consumer lines division (consumer lines means insurance for individual people, not companies) that used new technology and new sources of data to better predict customer behavior and improve top- and bottom-line results dramatically. Why didn't I say that? It would've taken under twelve seconds to share that information. David Herzog, our CFO, would have been greatly interested in what I was doing, because my improving results most certainly benefited the financial health of our organization. When the ride was done and those elevator doors opened on the twenty-seventh floor, he may have said, "Christine, I'd love to hear more about that. I'll send you a calendar invite—perhaps we can talk more about what you're doing."

Which brings me to my second point—I never gave him my last name, so how on earth would he have even found me if he wanted to talk further? Our first and last names help us to be unique. Please try and get into the habit of sharing your first and last names when you meet new people, so that you are more memorable and unique. I always do this now. Then my new acquaintances can find me in the company directory, on LinkedIn, or on attendee lists and reach out later to create more opportunities and wins.

I'd like you to develop your own elevator speech. I'll help you. When considering what you might share, think about who you are and what value you bring. This message may be different depending on if you're meeting a peer within your organization (like a colleague), a higher-up (your manager or the executive team), someone in your industry but outside your organization (a customer or vendor), or someone outside your industry (a neighbor or friend). You also need to consider what information might be appropriate to share inside your organization but must remain confidential from anyone else.

As an example of the varied approach, I might tell our CFO about building a new capability for the consumer lines division, but that information may not be compelling to the person I meet at the dinner party. Instead, I'll tell my dinner party acquaintance that I use data and computers to predict the timing and amounts of insurance claims in the US—and I'm finding ways to do that better and faster than anyone else. I might pivot slightly from both of these when meeting another actuary or a vendor, as an actuary or a vendor might find still other aspects of my work even more compelling.

Now it's your turn. Pages 144 and 145 are purposefully left blank, and I'd like you to pause, think about your work, and brainstorm the following:

▸ What do you do?

▸ What value do you bring to your organization?

▸ What value do you bring to your customers?

▸ What value do you bring to society?

▸ How do you do your job differently and perhaps better than others?

▸ How are your results different and perhaps better than others'?

▸ What positive feedback have you received about your work that could be incorporated into your value statement(s)?

▸ What parts of your job do you particularly enjoy?

Write down everything you can think of—it doesn't matter how big or how small or how incredible or how trivial. Your particular work may lend itself to other questions not listed above. As you write down your ideas, they will spark other, new ideas. Try to differentiate between the tasks that you do and the value that you bring. When considering your value, think about this from a couple points of view:

▸ Output or results that can be measured—for example, higher sales, lower expenses, better health, faster progress, streamlined operations, decreased turnover, improved customer satisfaction, less waste, higher scores. How are you contributing to these sorts of preferred measurable outcomes?

▸ Valuable qualities that you bring to your customers and organization through your work style—for example, do you add creativity and positivity? Do you bring your can-do attitude every day? Are you a selfless teacher or trainer within your group? Are you loyal and trustworthy?

Now that you have a long list of potential value phrases, see if you can narrow this list by identifying key ideas and eliminating the rest. The key ideas are the things that you believe make you interesting and compelling. When you look over your list, which ideas or phrases stand out to you as most noteworthy, significant, interesting, or unique? Which do you think might appeal to your varied audiences? Because your message might differ depending on your audience, you may wish to pull different sets of key ideas. Which ideas might appeal to a peer? A higher-up? A personal acquaintance?

Connect these key ideas and value statements into an introduction that has a natural flow. Make sure it is short but powerful. It might take a number of tries to develop something that sounds great. A thesaurus may help you find exactly the right words. If you feel awkward reading back your statement or think it sounds artificial, then give some further thought as to why you're passionate about your work. What parts of your work get you excited? Which parts are you proud of? Can you incorporate these points? If you're authentically sharing the aspects of your work that are compelling to *you*, then you will likely naturally convey that interest and excitement to your audience.

One area where many of us may have trouble is sharing our value without feeling like we're bragging. I feel that, too—in fact, when I began writing this book, I thought it was necessary to include the reasons that I was qualified to write it. My background and accomplishments were essential to the story, yet I struggled with how to do that in a way that was informational but not braggy. This was particularly difficult because I recognized that different readers will have different perspectives on what constitutes informational and what constitutes braggy. What do I include? What do I leave out? If

PART 3: ELEVATE YOURSELF

_____

_____

_____

_____

_____

_____

_____

_____

_____

_____

_____

_____

_____

_____

_____

_____

_____

_____

_____

_____

_____

_____

_____

_____

I leave too much out, do I appear unqualified? If I put too much in, do I look self-centered? I wrote the introduction to this book about twenty-five different ways. I then settled on one approach but asked my editor, Hannah, for her honest feedback. I asked her if and where I should soften any language, to ensure that my tone was balanced.

If you struggle with this, too, then look to your Hannahs—we all have Hannahs. They are our trusted colleagues or friends or family members who can help us to brainstorm ideas and be sure that our personal value statements sound balanced. Ask your Hannahs for feedback—and hear them. And also remember this: others who have surpassed us with promotions and recognition and accolades probably surpassed us because they found a way to have the strength and confidence to gracefully promote their own accomplishments. Remember that Roselyn said "thank you" while I deflected. We, too, must find the strength and confidence to gracefully share our accomplishments. Just take a deep breath and do it. Find your balance and go for it!

So at this point, you've written an introductory statement that you think might just work. I mentioned a balanced tone just now, so let's think for a moment about that. Something technical may be perfect or too stuffy. Something factual and concise may be wholly believable, or it may neglect to convey your personality and spark. Informal or nontechnical introductions could suggest energy and a personal connection, or they could leave your professionalism in question. The balance is important, and this is going to be different for everyone depending on your work, what you bring to the table, and your audience. (Consider the examples I provided earlier. They are probably more appropriate for an acquaintance than a peer within that example's industry, as you can tell from the generally nontechnical language and informal tone.)

Read your elevator speech out loud. How does it sound when you actually say it? One tip for practicing your elevator speech (or any planned remarks) is to leave your speech on your own voice mail or a voice-recorder app. Then you can listen to it and make any necessary improvements to your content or delivery. You want to develop and practice your elevator speech so that you can deliver it with ease and confidence whenever needed—during a chance encounter, a planned networking event, or an unplanned event. Practice in the car. Practice in the shower. Practice when you're home alone. Practice. Practice. Practice. You want to sound natural and comfortable. You want to be able to easily go into autopilot with your new value statement.

Overall—remember the goal. You're looking for a compelling value statement that replaces your previous one-word answer to "What do you do?" You're looking to keep the conversation open so the relationship can potentially flourish. Once you have your elevator speech down, you'll be able to share your value confidently, quickly, easily, and accurately. You'll strengthen your positive reputation and enhance your presence. You'll expand your impact.

COMMUNICATION BEYOND THE WORDS

I wrote above that "you want to sound natural and comfortable" and "share your value confidently." This is important because it turns out that the *words* you use in your elevator speech (and every time you communicate) are not the only source of information you're sharing about yourself. As you're delivering your thoughtful, well-written, well-rehearsed, value-based introduction, your vocal tones, body language, and facial expressions are also influencing your messaging.

That's because communication involves more than words. We learned earlier that our human tendency toward unintentional blindness developed over two million years ago as a survival mechanism. It turns out that communication through means other than the words themselves developed then, too. You see, early humans had undeveloped voices, and so they could only communicate through grunts and nonverbal gestures. These grunts and gestures became highly important for conveying information and intended messages. In the modern world, tones and gestures still heavily influence our communication, expressing additional information to our audiences.

Here's an example. Have you ever received a text that says "OK"? This two-letter phrase may be interpreted as:

That's fine with me.
No comment.
I read what you said and agree.
I read what you said and think that's completely ridiculous.
Great!
I'm mad at you.

Hmm. The confusion has arisen because tone, body language, and facial expression are not available in text. Text is words only. The introduction of emojis (small graphics or icons that are used to express emotion) and alternative punctuation (exclamation point! period. neither #?*) has helped somewhat convey tone in electronic communications like texts or tweets, but I'm sure many of us have at one time or another either misinterpreted the intention of a text— or been misinterpreted.

Let's explore the various communication cues (words, tone, body language, and facial expressions) so that we can be sure to build our winning conditions when we share our great value. Since these ideas relate to *all* communication (not just elevator speeches), I have not limited the descriptions and examples to value-based introductions only. You can and should think about these ideas for all of your workplace (and out-of-the-workplace) interactions.

The **words** you speak should be clear and precise. Your audience should understand what you are saying. Don't include highly technical or industry jargon unless your audience is fully capable of receiving information of this level and detail. Acronyms should be naturally understood or defined. Long, meandering, and run-on sentences could be confusing. If possible, try to keep your sentences direct and succinct. Avoid fillers (um, uh, er, like).

If you are not engaging in person (for example, if you're talking on the phone or over a webinar, WebEx, or Skype-type connection) then make sure you have a solid audio connection. Ultimately, your goal is for your words to be well heard and well understood.

Your **tone of voice** should mirror the context and content of your spoken words. Tone considers aspects such as emphasis, pitch, and pace. Tone is the mechanism that conveys whether you are serious or joking, happy or angry, excited or irritated. If your tone doesn't match the content of your words, then usually it's the tone—not the words—that is believed. For example, let's pretend that you're under a tight deadline. You state that you'll comfortably complete the work, but you say these words in a high-pitched, fast, frantic, neurotic way. Despite your words, your manager may expect you to miss the deadline.

Have you ever nicely asked someone to do something, and they grumbled or mumbled angrily under their breath, "Oh, all right"? How did that make you feel? You probably felt like they didn't want to do that task. Even though the words *oh, all right* indicated acceptance, the grumbled, angry tone suggested otherwise. (This exact situation may or may not happen in my house as relates to the unloading of the dishwasher . . .)

Have you ever casually answered the phone, "Hello?" and heard the caller immediately say, "What's wrong!?" These are all examples of tone communicating something other than the words themselves. Since tone may be relied upon more heavily than words, be mindful that your tone is conveying the feelings and information that you wish to convey.

Your **body language** adds even more information beyond your words and tone. Body language includes your posture, gestures, and eye contact. Are you calm and still, or are you fidgety? Are you looking at the person with whom you're speaking, or are you looking away or down? Are your eyes darting all around? Are your arms on your hips, or at your sides, or crossed across your chest? How long do you delay before responding?

Body language that suggests confidence and friendliness includes direct eye contact, leaning forward slightly to indicate your interest and attention, and standing or sitting up straight with an open posture. Try not to fidget (spinning your pen, shaking your foot, tapping your fingers, checking your phone). Keep your head up. Smile. Don't slouch or clench your fists.

My family and I were recently watching the game show *Jeopardy!* and one of the three contestants was standing at the podium with their arms crossed. They looked completely closed off and disengaged. Perhaps uninterested. They didn't win, and we weren't surprised, because their body language suggested that they didn't care very much.

Think about your **facial expressions**. Be aware of the message that your face is sending. Do you know anyone who is usually scowling? Or someone who is usually smiling and appears eager to learn? Which of these do you want to convey? Take one second right now and think about the expression you have on your face at this exact moment. Are you smiling or scowling? Are you conveying interest, or boredom, or happiness, or anger? Recognize that if you are in a room with other people, they have read that on your face.

For better or worse, people begin judging you the moment you enter the room, before you even have an opportunity to begin speaking. So be mindful that your body language and facial expressions provide the right information about you to others. Have you ever walked into a room full of people, taken a quick glance around, and immediately noticed that one dynamic, charismatic person who just exudes confidence and magnetism by simply standing there? That is nonvocal communication at its best.

Meetings are an ideal opportunity to notice the impact of nonvocal means of communication. As you look around the table, you will sense who is most (or least) engaged simply by their behavior and posture. Is anyone repeatedly checking their phone? Fidgeting?

Doodling? Looking around instead of at the speaker? Regardless of how they actually feel, this person *appears* to be less engaged. Are there others who are leaning forward, looking directly at the speaker, and taking notes? These people appear to be highly engaged.

A few years ago, I worked with a young professional who never brought a notepad or pencil to a meeting. Now, they were brilliant— they probably had a photographic memory and so didn't need a pen or paper—but these actions gave the *impression* that they were not engaged. I pulled them aside and gently told them that even if they never wrote down a single word, the mere existence of the pad and pencil at a meeting implies interest. From that day forward, they always showed up with a pad and pencil. What message do you want to be sending?

Winning conditions is becoming consciously aware of the message you're sending through all means of communication—not only your words, but also your tone, body language, and facial expression. Make sure these elements are in sync to ensure that your audience doesn't misinterpret whatever you're intending to communicate. Now you can see why practicing your elevator speech (or any planned remarks) in advance can benefit you tremendously. You will not only perfect your words, but practice will help your tone and body language to also convey a sense of ease, confidence, friendliness, comfort, and conviction. You will be able to more fully share your value with the world.

So go share your value with the world!

VIRTUAL INTRODUCTIONS

But hold on—before we move on, we need to cover one more area. We don't meet all of our connections in face-to-face encounters. In fact, the potential for virtual introductions has skyrocketed, and so we need to be sure that our electronic introductions also thoughtfully promote our great value. Think about social media platforms like LinkedIn. If you're on LinkedIn, then you have a headline, which is the 120-character description under your name. How do you describe yourself? Pretend this is your virtual elevator speech. Does it tell the world your value? If only your job title is listed there, then go back to your brainstormed list and see what you can add. So you're a sales manager. What else? How are you outstanding? Do you bring vitality and results to the sales process through motivating leadership and a commitment to integrity? Did you increase sales by x percent? What new products did you bring to market? How much expense did you save while keeping sales at their record high levels? Do you lead a team? Figure out what sets you apart and add that to your bio. Try not to be hokey—every once in a while a "data evangelist" will try to connect with me, and I don't even know what that means. Definitely don't peruse your degree. ☺

Just like you have different (spoken) elevator speeches for varied audiences, you may have different headlines for varied social media. My personal Twitter bio is different from my LinkedIn headline, simply because my followers are different and I bring separate value to each. But they are both important, so please double-check and optimize whatever you're putting out there into the world.

Take a look at your résumé. Does it simply list your positions and dates worked and responsibilities without sharing all of the incredibly valuable things you did? Add your value!

The point is, you are more than your profession. You are more than your role. You are more than your team. You are bringing value to your work every day, and it's up to you to share your worth. Don't expect others to automatically know what you do—you'll need to graciously tell them.

In the next chapter, we'll take our discussion of words, tone, and body language a bit further and apply these to creating a sense of magnetism, because if your colleagues are drawn to you, then they will want to help you succeed.

CHAPTER 10

BE
MAGNETIC

Have you been on a job interview recently? Conversation about anything personal is usually completely off-limits for legal and ethical reasons, so many interviews can be pretty standard. Candidates can often expect the usual barrage of:

Why are you looking for a new position?
What are your strengths?
Tell me about a recent challenge and how you overcame it.
How did you hear about this position?

Those are pretty boring for the interviewer as well. So some interviewers are getting creative and asking questions that are decidedly outside of the box. My husband was recently interviewed for a new position and received this question:

What is your favorite television commercial?

The role itself had absolutely nothing to do with television. Or commercials.

I've interviewed probably a hundred professionals throughout my career, and my impressions have run the gamut from "Wow, I like this person a lot. How soon can we extend an offer?" to "I don't like this person at all. How soon can we wrap it up?" Oh, I feel like I've seen it all. I've interviewed candidates who have researched my entire background on the internet before meeting me, and others who have no idea what's even happening and call me by the wrong name. I've interviewed candidates who are fully professional and appropriate, and others who think their frat house stories are acceptable to share in an office environment with someone they've just met (this time talking about Pika, not PICA). I've interviewed candidates who want the position desperately and are fully engaged, and others who seem remarkably uninterested and . . . wait for it . . . yawn. No, the yawner was not working a night job to support the new baby, nor working around the clock to finish a consulting project with motivation, dedication, and a commitment to excellence. Nope, they were just trying to be cool by acting standoffish. Not cool.

I interviewed a candidate once on Halloween. I wouldn't have ordinarily scheduled an interview on Halloween, because I enjoy dressing up for our office costume parties. But this was the only day that worked for the candidate, and we were trying to accommodate his schedule. I showed up to the interview dressed as the bride of Frankenstein, complete with beehive wig, full face of horror makeup, and my actual nineteen-year-old wedding gown. The formally and appropriately dressed candidate took two steps into our interview room and promptly told me that he was wearing a Superman T-shirt under his interview suit, à la Clark Kent. That was a great interview. I liked the candidate a lot. His skills were strong, his background was impressive, and his work ethic was clear. I extended him an offer.

Because I have interviewed so many candidates throughout my career, I am often asked by my colleagues, "Whom do I hire? What do I look for in a candidate?" Well, there's the obvious requirement of demonstrating the skills and experience necessary to perform the job functions well. But beyond that, I look for candidates who are dedicated, motivated, creative, understanding, honest, and flexible. I look for candidates whose backgrounds allow them to provide a diversity of thought, experience, and perspective that will complement the rest of the team. I look for candidates who exhibit positive leadership and thoughtful collaboration. These are the candidates I hire.

With colleagues on Halloween and yes, I interviewed a candidate dressed like this.

So how is it possible that in a short thirty-minute interview, some candidates are able to imply these desirable qualities, while others do not? Well, we've already learned that proactively and thoughtfully expressing personal value can positively impact outcomes (don't forget to prepare your elevator speech!). But in addition to this, there are situational and behavioral elements that we can control, that can help other people to actually *like* us more. It's possible to actively create a sense of personal charisma. We can take steps that inspire other people to want to be around us—and to want us to be around. We can make ourselves magnetic. Just like a magnet produces an invisible force that pulls objects toward itself, you can create the conditions by which people are drawn to you.

This is important, because we're more likely to want to work with magnetic people. When we like someone, we're more likely to listen to, recognize, and celebrate them. We're more likely to give them the benefit of the doubt and excuse their mistakes. We may think that the things they're doing are better than they may actually be. When we're drawn to someone, we'll often do what we can to help them succeed.

Back in Chapter 3, we talked about the importance of building a coalition of advocates. The larger your support crew, the more likely you are to succeed. We learned that people tend to support work that improves their current positioning and resist work that deteriorates their positioning. That discussion related entirely to how people view the actual work product itself. Here we push this idea further. You see, people tend to support *people* they're drawn to, and tend to resist people that are off-putting. By building preference around not only our work, but also ourselves, we can effectively increase our likelihood of hire, promotion, recognition, selection, callback, forgiveness for error, or any other win. Winning conditions is being magnetic.

So let's talk, then, about some proven ways that we can effectively increase our magnetism.

Now, clearly the first rule of being magnetic is "don't be a jerk."

But this is obvious, so I'm not even going there. I already assume that you're a nice person with good and honest intentions. You already know to avoid highly controversial discussion topics in the workplace and to never engage in any insulting or mocking conversations or comments toward people based on their race, religion, gender, sexual orientation, family or financial status, or other demographics. What we'll cover in this chapter are a couple of ways to help an already likable person—like you—be even more magnetic. (Note, because spelling can be tricky, "likable" or "likability" refers to the act of liking someone—thinking that they're pleasant and enjoyable to be around. We are not talking about licking a person. Some people may be both likable and lickable, but that is outside the scope of this book.)

WORDS, TONE, AND GESTURES

We learned in the last chapter that communication may be vocal (words and tone) or nonvocal (body language and facial expression). Both vocal and nonvocal cues communicate information to your audience. It turns out that these cues also influence liking.

Back in the late 1960s, psychology professor Albert Mehrabian conducted a series of experiments to better understand how words, tone, and facial expressions impact our feelings or opinions about other people. Results suggested that only a small percentage of how much we like a person is actually based on the content of what they say. It turns out that facial expressions and tone can impact our opinions much more. Said differently, it's not just what we say but how we say it. What's important is how we make people feel. So if you want to draw people in—regardless of your message—then be sure that your tone and gestures help create that positive feeling.

In its simplest form, we can break down this idea into four situations:

1. Sharing a positive message in a positive way. This is winning conditions. Consider the interviews. I might interview multiple candidates on the same day who all say exactly the same words:

"I'm interested in this position."
"I'm fully qualified to complete the work well."
"Yes, I'm a team player."
"I am responsible."

So whom do I prefer? I prefer the candidates whose tone and gestures support them being:

interested in the position,
fully qualified to complete the work well,
a team player,
responsible.

These are candidates whose tone is positive, friendly, and engaging. Their body language is confident and attentive. They smile. These positive tones and positive gestures make me believe that they are honest, committed, responsible team players. I trust their words, and I am drawn in. The converse of this is:

2. Sharing a positive message in a negative way. This is not winning conditions. Have you ever been right in the middle of a good conversation with someone when they suddenly begin to do something else, like look through papers or get their coat? How does this make you feel? You probably don't like it. You may feel as if the person is no longer interested in talking with you. It doesn't matter what's being said, because you *see* their focus shift to something else, and that feels negative.

Think about the candidate who yawned. Very interested in the position? Nah—probably not. In fact, any tones or gestures that indicate:

lack of interest in the position,
not qualified to complete the work well,
not a team player,
irresponsible

are going to cause some dislike, even if your words told me something different. The negative tone and gestures undermine the positive assertions. It's the opposite of magnetic—it's off-putting.

We can extend these ideas beyond interviews and into the workplace itself. Actions that could inadvertently undermine your excellent work include being late for work or meetings, checking your phone or social media frequently (unless required for your position), looking bored or disengaged, behaving inappropriately, and using angry or overly emotional tones when speaking. Perhaps your work is excellent, but if your tones and gestures cause people to not like you so much, then you may not achieve those positive outcomes for which you're striving.

3. Sharing a negative message in a positive way. Curiously, this is also winning conditions. Because gestures and tone can impact how we make a person feel—more than the words we say—if we need to deliver some bad news, we should deliver that news in a thoughtful, kind, considerate, empathetic way. Consider the tactics we learned to use if our work will deteriorate someone's positioning. We learned to communicate with empathy and understanding. We learned to help people feel respected despite the change. Now we understand why these tactics work—because sometimes it's not what we say, but how we say it. If you treat other people with respect and can create a sense of magnetism through positive tone and gestures, then they are more likely to support you even if you're delivering a negative message.

Note that "a positive way" is described here as "thoughtful, kind, considerate, empathetic," and "respectful." It's not described as fake, cloying, or saccharine. "A positive way" doesn't mean "plaster a fake smile on your face and go deliver the news"—which would only serve to create feelings of skepticism or distrust. Instead, you want to handle the communication honestly and authentically. Ensuring that your tone and expressions are respectful, thoughtful, and kind will enable you to deliver a difficult message without coming across as condescending or belittling.

4. Sharing a negative message in a negative way. Losing conditions. This is bulldozing your colleagues into compliance when your work impacts them negatively and you don't care. They won't like your work or you. It's a lose-lose.

Overall, keeping your tone and body language authentically positive while you engage with your audience will help to increase your magnetism.

THE HALO EFFECT

I once had a colleague who was incredibly smart and also creative. Whatever the business problem, they always seemed to be able to develop exactly the right solution that was both practical and precise. Their work was dependably accurate, on time, and thorough. Their direct reports spoke highly of their leadership style. Yet their promotions came less frequently than expected. Others with similar years of service (or even fewer) were moved into more senior-level positions. Year-end performance ratings didn't peg them as a top performer. This might have seemed curious or confusing . . . until you took even the briefest glance into their office.

That office was in an alarming state. There were stacks of papers everywhere. Every inch of desk space and more than half the floor was covered in piles of outdated documents, newspapers, and files. One corner of the room contained old takeout cartons and half-full cans of soda. Next to the desk were several pairs of worn-out sneakers and a couple of stained sweatshirts. This office could have been featured on an episode of *Hoarders*.

My colleague had been asked on more than one occasion to clean out their office. It bordered on being both a health and fire hazard. And yet they laughed off these requests and claimed they knew where everything was. They didn't want to risk throwing out something they might need. It may *appear* disorganized, you see, but actually there was a system. The rest of us might not understand that system, but nonetheless, there wasn't a problem.

Except there was. You see, the consequence of a disorganized, messy, or chaotic work space goes beyond the work space itself. It can actually impact how other people view your work and view you. That's because our predictably irrational human brains will sometimes observe one concrete characteristic and then apply this characteristic or judgment across other dimensions. In this case, because the office was disorganized and chaotic, my colleague's work may have been assumed to also contain an element of disorganization and chaos. Was this an accurate judgment? Perhaps not. Was this the reason that they weren't promoted? Maybe. Judgments happen when our human brains take shortcuts.

But this isn't always bad news, because we can leverage the shortcut to our advantage. You see, if we know that our predictably irrational human brains might observe one concrete characteristic and then apply this judgment across other dimensions, then we can take steps to ensure that the observed characteristic is positive. Said another way, if you present yourself in a way that is professional, organized, and appropriate, then your work is more likely to be assumed to be professional, organized, and appropriate. It's called the *halo effect*—named by psychologist Edward Thorndike in reference to someone having a halo. And we can *create* halos—or positive characteristics—to increase our magnetism.

Consider your work space. Make sure it's orderly, clean, and consistently professional. Putting away your passwords, confidential files or papers, and any sensitive data assets will support your being focused and having integrity. Wash your empty coffee mug and toss your empty food containers. Smelly gym clothes belong in a bag, out of view and out of scent. Keeping your space fresh will support your being approachable and open to collaboration. Make sure that your personal effects like photographs and other decor are office appropriate. You may have had a raging good time at Oktoberfest last year, but the photo of you wasted and swinging from the chandelier with a giant beer stein might not be the best image to introduce to colleagues. The photo of you wrapped up in your golden retriever, or blowing out birthday candles with your child, or graduating from college or high school is probably a better choice. While not everyone may agree that a cluttered desk indicates a cluttered mind, you don't want to risk creating a negative impression when it's relatively easy to create a positive one.

You can also create halos beyond your desk space. Think about your emails. They should be easy to read, navigate, and digest, not rambling all over the place without headings or structure. Think about your social media. Posts and profiles should be inviting and well written, without run-on sentences or atrocious punctuation. Any public photos and information that you include should be appropriate. Think about your website design. It should be attractive and easy to navigate, without spelling errors or circular references. Each of these will foster positive feelings about your work and about you.

Create halos about your own personal presence by making sure that you and your clothes are clean and appropriately groomed. Dress appropriately for your position. Brush your teeth. Smile. Avoid heavy perfumes and strong odors from last night's dinner. Stand tall with good posture. Caring about your entire professional presence suggests that you also care about your work. It's a simple way to draw others in.

POSITIVE ASSOCIATIONS

We can push this idea of Thorndike's halo effect a bit further. Here's an example. What do you think of when you hear the word

Clydesdale? Many people think of Budweiser. Clydesdale horses were originally gifted to the CEO of Budweiser in 1933 to celebrate the end of Prohibition, and since then, they've remained an iconic representation of Budweiser beer. They've been celebrated in Super Bowl commercials almost every year since 1986, and with good reason. They make our hearts swell. They make us feel good. We like them.

Now granted, a horse has absolutely nothing to do with beer. But in this case our brains do something like this:

I see a beautiful horse. → I like the horse. → The horse is associated with beer. → Therefore I must also like the beer.

Look familiar? This path is reminiscent of the same shortcut our brains take when we perceive a positive characteristic (a well-organized work space) and apply that positive judgment to your work or work style (you are focused, approachable, and open to collaboration). Here, we apply our positive feelings about the horse to the product with which the horse is associated. I like the horse, therefore I must like the beer. Budweiser has created a *winning association*.

We can use the same technique to maximize our winning conditions. Back in the 1980s, marketing professor Dr. Robert Cialdini became quite well-known for his research into the science of persuasion. One of the things Cialdini found through his research is that an association with good (positive) things will positively influence how others feel about us. So if we purposefully connect our ideas with positive associations, then our business partners will be more drawn to us and to our ideas. (Incidentally, Cialdini's research also formed the backbone of the next two concepts in this chapter.)

For example, it's been shown that people become fonder of other people and ideas when they're having a meal together. I like the meal, therefore I must also like you and your idea. The common name for this concept—the *luncheon technique*—was coined by psychologist Gregory Razran. Every consultant everywhere seems to leverage the luncheon technique, and for good reason—it works. This is the same idea behind meetings on the golf course or conferences in Las Vegas. *I like playing golf, so I like you and I like your work. I am having fun in Vegas, so I like you and I like your work.* It's positive association.

Positive association is why community service team-building events are so successful. When we work together at a soup kitchen or build a home for Habitat for Humanity, we feel good about giving back to our communities. Therefore, we feel good about our colleagues. Realtors might suggest that home sellers burn cookie-scented candles, because many home buyers associate warm cookies with comfort, family, and happy occasions. Organizations that host CPR training are not only teaching useful skills, but are also drawing employees together—*I feel so great about my CPR training that I also feel great about you.*

Some people will add the title of the book they're reading, or their favorite quote, to their email signature. *I like that book, too—now I like you! What an inspiring quote—you are inspiring!* I've heard of teams blasting a motivating song before a big meeting, just to get the attendees psyched up about the project at hand. Others might get started with more relaxing music to introduce a sense of calm, ease, and order. Some teams or colleagues might wear red on Fridays to support our troops or wear pink during October to support breast cancer awareness. Each of these creates magnetism simply from a positive association. What positive association can you create with your work in your organization?

While you want to aim for positive associations, you also want to be mindful of avoiding negative associations. Have you ever heard the phrase *don't shoot the messenger?* This phrase cautions people to not automatically blame the deliverer of bad news. It's a valid caution, since our predictably irrational human brains could just have easily made this shortcut on the path to understanding:

To avoid negative association, remember that sharing a negative message in an authentically positive way can boost your magnetism. Be thoughtful, kind, considerate, and empathetic. Help people to feel respected. Consider the situation from their point of view.

PULLING TOGETHER TOWARD A COMMON GOAL

Recently there was a news story out of Arkansas in which a six-year-old child was hit by a car and became trapped underneath. Bystanders came immediately to the child's rescue and worked cooperatively to lift the four-thousand-pound automobile off them. The child was saved, only suffering minor burns and cuts. Despite the awful accident, the community felt a sense of unity, harmony, and attachment. There was an outpouring of love.

In this case, the community members worked together toward a shared vision—saving the life of the child. The harmony that was felt following the incident was the result of their pulling together toward a common goal. It's the idea that "We're all in this together."

Pulling together heightens the exposure effect. You'll remember that the exposure effect suggests that the more often you are exposed to something, the more your brain likes it, and then the more likely you are to say yes to it. Well, you can actually amplify the exposure effect if you include an element of cooperation while creating your repeated contact points. You want to find a way to work together toward a shared future vision. You can reinforce this mutual cooperation by verbally acknowledging that you are working together:

I'm looking forward to solving this with you.
It's great to work together on this.
Our goals are fully aligned.

My sister Ellen is a former labor and delivery nurse, and she had a beautiful experience with a patient that perfectly highlights this idea of establishing a strong magnetic bond by working together toward a common goal. Early in her career, Ellen was caring for a Jewish woman who wanted more than anything to have a Pidyon Ha'Ben ceremony for her firstborn baby—a boy. This holy ceremony is quite uncommon—only one in ten families meet all the conditions. One of these conditions is that it may be observed only for a firstborn son who "opened his mother's womb,"[10] which means the baby was delivered vaginally, not by caesarean section. Unfortunately the mom's labor had stalled, and her obstetrician had warned that a C-section was probably imminent. The young mom wasn't much older than my sister, and Ellen felt a deep compassion for her.

Ellen knew that squatting, instead of the more traditional birthing position of lying on your back, could sometimes help a stalled labor to progress. She also knew that this was largely unconventional in a hospital setting. Nonetheless, with the doctor's approval, my sister helped the young mom to her feet. She helped her squat. She held her and waited with her and comforted her through her contractions. She reminded her that she wasn't leaving her side. She told her she was with her through this delivery. They were in this together.

And then, well, not too long later, that beautiful firstborn healthy baby, a son, he opened his mother's womb. What a glorious moment for those two young women! They had worked together toward a common goal. And on the thirty-first day after the child's birth, my sister attended the child's Pidyon Ha'Ben ceremony. The young mom has sent my sister a thank-you card every year since on the boy's birthday. He is now twenty-five years old.

Work together toward a common goal. By the way, this is why asking for help can often be viewed as a sign of strength, not weakness. The collaboration positively influences liking. Now, this only

---

10 Rabbi Shraga Simmons, "Pidyon Ha'Ben – Redemption of First Born," aish.com, July 6, 2002, https://www.aish.com/jl/l/b/Pidyon_Haben_-_Redemption_of_First_Born.html?mobile=yes.

takes effect if you are working *together*. Asking for help simply so the other person can do the work for you isn't collaborating. But if you can find the right balance, you will have enhanced your winning conditions.

What will you help your colleagues accomplish? How can they help you?

SIMILARITY

Have you ever been driving down the highway and noticed a window cling on a nearby car's window that celebrated the college or high school that you attended? Or perhaps it's a bumper sticker of a dog breed (*my dog is the same breed!*) or local gym (*I work out at that gym, too!*). If so, then you're more likely to feel an affinity to the stranger driving that car. Maybe you let them in front of you when the traffic is backed up or smile at them as you drive by. You do this because similarity breeds liking. We are drawn to people with whom we share commonalities. You saw the bumper sticker, you have something in common, so you like them.

You can leverage this idea in the workplace to build your magnetism. In fact, finding a similarity or two with your colleagues before getting down to business is a great way to improve your outcomes, because it creates a *feeling* of familiarity. We've learned through the exposure effect that familiarity breeds acceptance, which can lead to preference. So, finding similarities will help to create that sense of charisma or preference.

Similarity could mean enjoying the same activities, television shows, movies, or sports. Maybe you have kids of similar ages or the same brand car. Maybe you've traveled to the same states or countries. Perhaps you both grew up out west or back east, or both studied journalism or nutrition or psychology. Consider the candidate I interviewed while dressed as the bride of Frankenstein. The candidate exploited this concept perfectly. Just two steps into the interview room, he vocalized a similarity—he told me he was also wearing a costume.

Note that when we talk about seeking similarity, we are *not* talking about the opposite of diversity. Research has consistently shown that diverse groups usually develop better solutions and outcomes than homogenous groups. Thus, organizations should absolutely strive to build teams comprised of different backgrounds, demographics, preferences, training, and opinions. In fact, if organizations lean on a mindset of creating similarity—either consciously or unconsciously—to unfairly discriminate against people based on their race, religion, sex, age, sexual orientation, or other protected status, then this would be not only totally unacceptable but also illegal. The goal here is to seek out similar interests that might pull us together amid our great diversity. What do you have in common with your colleagues?

If you can't (or don't want to) *find* a similarity, you can *create* one by mirroring your colleagues' speech patterns, body language, and tone. By "mirror" I don't mean copy every gesture to the point where you're making a mockery of the situation or being disingenuous. I simply mean, if your colleague is more formal, then tend toward formal—don't greet them with a high five, a "hey!" or a hug. If they're chatty, then be chatty. If they speak softly, then leave your outside voice outside.

Now, you'll only want to mirror behaviors that satisfy the professional norms of the organization (for example, don't be chatty if that's inappropriate—even if your colleague is chatty). And you also shouldn't mirror behaviors that make you uncomfortable or fall outside your own personal values or beliefs. Once, at the conclusion of an interview, I extended my hand to the candidate for a handshake. She declined because her religious beliefs prohibited it. Her decision to *not* shake in this case wasn't a deterrent for me—in fact, it positively illustrated her adherence to values. (Beyond extending my hand, I also ended up extending an offer.)

Companies can create similarities by sharing information about charitable or societal causes that customers may also support. Perhaps a company is environmentally friendly or socially responsible. Perhaps products are cruelty-free. Do you also support these causes? If so, then you are more likely to be drawn to that company.

The flip side of "similarity breeds liking" means that dissimilarity could potentially breed disliking. To that end, be careful when presenting particularly divisive or contentious non-work-related opinions. These could alienate your business partners and negatively impact your success. You may also want to be mindful of strong opinions that you express outside the workplace, like on public social media sites.

ABOVE ALL ELSE, BE TRUE TO YOURSELF

We've learned that we're more likely to want to work with magnetic people. When we like someone and want to be around them, we're more likely to listen to and celebrate them. We're more likely to give them the benefit of the doubt. When we're drawn to someone, we'll often do what we can to help them succeed.

The good news is, it's possible to actively create personal charisma and make ourselves magnetic. Remember to:

▸ make sure that your tone and gestures are authentic and positive,

▸ take care with how you present yourself and your work space,

▸ purposefully connect your ideas with winning associations,

▸ find a way to work together with your colleagues toward a common goal, and

▸ find similarities amid wonderful diversity.

But before we close this chapter, it's important that I explicitly and clearly articulate that as you are taking these steps to maximize your magnetism, you should never, ever compromise your own standards. Let me repeat that.

Do not compromise your standards.

If someone tells an inappropriate joke or makes derogatory comments, then please don't mirror and match. If someone is behaving in a way that runs against typical and acceptable standards of behavior, then do not cooperate with this poor behavior just to make them like you more. When looking for commonalities with a colleague, do not misrepresent your opinions, preferences, and hobbies to try to match their interests. In fact, just like I was drawn to the candidate who didn't shake my hand, authenticity and standing up for your own values can often add its own element of magnetism.

Remember I told you about that toxic work environment? One day I was approached in the hallway by an executive far more senior than me, and he asked me condescendingly if I was wearing my daughter's clothes. Then he laughed right in my face. I had no idea what he was talking about, until he added, "Your sweater—it looks like Garanimals! Ha-ha!"

Now, for those of you who aren't familiar with Garanimals, they are mix-and-match clothing pieces for young children. The tag on each item displays a picture of an animal. A small child will know what tops and bottoms go together by matching the animals on the tags.

Well, it took about two seconds for me to realize that this jerk was making fun of my gray cashmere sweater, which displayed a simple graphic of a duck. I'll tell you what I did *not* do:

▸ I did not stop wearing the sweater in order to break the expressed negative association.

▸ I did not laugh at his joke or mirror and match his mocking behavior.

▸ I did not in any way cooperate with this degrading treatment.

Instead, I looked him in the eye, calmly told him that his words were highly inappropriate, turned around, and walked back to my desk. From that day forward, every time I had a meeting with the executive, I made sure that I was wearing my duck sweater. Because staying true to myself and my values—liking myself—was winning conditions.

Let's continue with this idea of staying ethically strong. In the next chapter, we'll explore the benefits of maintaining your integrity and treating others with kindness and respect. Here we go.

CHAPTER 11

CELEBRATE KINDNESS AND INTEGRITY

A bout seven or eight years into my career, I was working on a project for a large international oil company that aimed to create more substantial retirement benefits for service station attendants (these are the people who pump gasoline into your car). At this point I was managing a small group of actuaries, and I thought that each person on my team was incredible. But there was one young actuary who particularly stood out to me. They were smart, dedicated, driven, and simply a joy to work with. They brought their A game to work every day. They worked super hard on this particular project, and I felt that their efforts were a big part of the reason that we carried it so successfully across the finish line.

When it came time to present final results to our firm's top management, I lauded this actuary in front of the group. I explicitly thanked them for their hard work, creativity, and dedication to the deadlines. I shared that their substantial contributions built the foundation for this project's success and that they were a real asset to our organization. My compliment was heartfelt and genuine. They had done an outstanding job, and it was important to me that others knew their value.

About a week or so later, the two of us were in another meeting together, discussing a different project with a completely different team of higher-ups. At one point during the discussion, the young actuary paid me a compliment back. They explained that my guidance had been critical to their learning process on this project and that I had really helped them to think outside the box. They told that group of higher-ups that they felt lucky to be able to work with me and learn from me. They said that I was a real asset to our team and our organization. I was of course grateful to hear their kind words, but I also wondered, "Had I been the beneficiary of reciprocity?"

RECIPROCITY

Reciprocity is the exchange of something for mutual benefit, such as privileges, small gifts, recognition, or favors. In social psychology, reciprocity refers to the act of rewarding kindness with kindness. In its alternate state, reciprocity can include responding to hostility with hostility. Essentially, we humans often feel obliged to respond in kind. In this case, I was curious if the compliment from my colleague was correlated to the compliment I had imparted previously. Or were these completely independent events, and the timing was simply coincidental? Was their compliment genuine and truly the result of my exceptional guidance, or had I somehow influenced their comments with my previous public accolade of their work?

I decided to test and learn. Over the next few weeks, I became consciously aware of the occasions when I paid my colleagues compliments or did small favors for them. These favors and compliments were still always authentic and heartfelt, but I was no longer mindless about it. I paid attention. And I noticed that the more good things I did for my colleagues, the more good things they did back for me. If I offered to help someone finish a project that was up against a tight deadline, usually they helped me back. When I paid someone a compliment, usually they paid me a compliment back. I wasn't thinking this was good karma, which is the age-old idea that when we put goodness out into the universe, then goodness comes back to us. Instead, I was thinking that this must be another predictable response of our human brains.

It turns out I was right. There have been a number of studies on reciprocity, but one of the most well-known was conducted in a restaurant by researchers David Strohmetz, Bruce Rind, Reed Fisher, and Michael Lynn.[11] The goal was to understand if a "gift" from the waiter had a positive correlation with the size of the tip. Or, more broadly, when given a gift, do humans feel compelled to reciprocate by giving a gift back? The answer is decidedly yes.

In the experiment, the baseline group of customers received the bill from the waiter without fanfare. The bill was simply delivered to the table with a thank-you and a smile. For another group of customers, the waiter delivered a small gift with the bill—just one small candy for each diner. In this case, the average tip increased by about 3 percent. If the waiter delivered two candies for each diner, then tips increased by about 14 percent. If the waiter delivered one candy, walked a few steps away, but then turned around and added a second candy, then the tips increased by about 21 percent. (Think about this the next time you are provided "free" after-dinner drinks, cookies, or . . . candy. How does this affect the tip that you leave the waitstaff or the review that you provide on Yelp?)

Studies on reciprocity have been numerous and varied, and the results have been remarkably consistent. When given a gift, humans feel compelled to give something back. This response may be conscious or subconscious, but either way, we tend to do it. We give back. If you are kind, then I am kind. If you are hostile, then I am hostile. If you do something for me, then I'll do something back for you. There go our human brains again!

But here's the rub—some people have learned how to exploit this basic human tendency for their own benefit. That is, they give

11 D. B. Strohmetz, B. Rind, R. Fisher, and M. Lynn. "Sweetening the till: The use of candy to increase restaurant tipping." *Journal of Applied Social Psychology*, 32, 2002. p. 300–309.

something purposefully (knowingly), so that the receiver gives back naturally. It's a trick. You think that's bad? I do, too. Keep reading, because it gets worse. Reciprocity in itself suggests a one-to-one gift, but the overachievers of the world took reciprocity to a whole new level with the development of a concept called pregiving.

Just like it sounds, pregiving is the act of giving to someone in advance. In advance of what? Well, this is where pregiving differs from reciprocity. In reciprocity, we give intentionally and then expect to get something back in short order. An eye for an eye. We look for the immediate payoff. In pregiving, we purposefully give small gifts or favors or compliments often, over time. The gifts may not result in immediate return, but eventually, our gifts or favors or compliments produce the results we were seeking. Eventually we get that positive return. So proponents of pregiving suggest that you give, and you give often. Keep giving! Give more!

Now, some people naturally give gifts and compliments often, simply because they enjoy doing so, but that is not the same as the concept of pregiving. Pregiving is done *with the express goal of eventually receiving something in return*. The whole purpose is the payoff. You do it to manipulate someone into doing or giving something back. There is selfish intent. And if this makes you feel icky— if you think this may be somewhat unscrupulous—then I'd probably agree with you. In fact, this whole idea of giving not out of goodness, but simply to get something back—like recognition, a sale, a promotion, anything—seems to me to be a little bit of trickery. To me, it's inauthentic. It's fake. It's Jedi mind tricks at work. It seems to me to lack integrity.

Others agree. In fact, in an effort to avoid potential manipulation through reciprocity or pregiving, some industries and organizations have actually revised the rules around permissible gifts. For example, in the medical education space, which aims to educate physicians on updated drug dosages, treatment plans, and prescribing trends, many educational conferences are no longer able to be held in locations that include the word *resort* in the name.

Such conferences have been relegated to mostly "airport hotels." The idea is that the conference sponsor—which is usually a pharmaceutical company—cannot provide gifts (i.e., luxurious accommodations or perceived vacations) to the physicians. Otherwise, physicians might consciously or unconsciously increase prescriptions for the meeting sponsor's pharmaceuticals. In many other industries and organizations, any gifts over twenty-five dollars (or some other nominal amount) must be formally reported and tracked. This ensures complete ethical transparency in decisioning with business partners. (Think about this if you're considering implementing a fancy event or a gift as part of a positive association.)

But let's turn back to my example at the top of the chapter. You'll remember that the more I gave, the more I got back. The more favors and compliments I imparted on my colleagues, the more they did back for me. It made me wonder, what's wrong with that? Weren't we all better off in the end? The answer is: yes, sometimes, maybe, and not necessarily. Hmm. Let's check out some more research, and then we'll put all this new knowledge together to understand our best options for creating winning conditions.

MORALITY AND ETHICS

In 2015, the University of California, Berkeley, released research[12] that sought to understand the impact of virtues and vices on influence. Virtues are behaviors that are considered to show high moral standards. These are desirable qualities, illustrating strength of character and respectability. Vices are behaviors that may be considered immoral or corrupt, or to have negative influence. Vices are weaknesses of character. The idea of the study was to understand if the display of positive or negative behaviors ultimately impacted

---

12 ten Brinke, Leanne, Christopher Liu, Dacher Keltner, and Sameer Srivastava. "Virtues, Vices, and Political Influence in the U.S. Senate." *Psychological Science* 27 (2016): 85–93. https://rady. ucsd.edu/docs/Virtues_ten%20Brinke%20Liu%20Keltner%20and%20Srivastava%202015.pdf

levels of power of influence in the workplace. And here, the study looked not at *perceived* power, but actual power. That is, were those exhibiting virtues or vices actually able to successfully collaborate and work toward measurable positive outcomes or positive change?

In the study, the body language, facial expressions, gestures, and tones displayed in the political speeches of more than 150 senators over a ten-year period were examined to infer the presence of virtues or vices. Virtuous traits including wisdom, courage, humanity, and justice were observed through behaviors such as eyebrows knit in concentration, sympathetic tones of voice, and the use of humor. Vices such as psychopathy, entitlement, narcissism, and emotional detachment were observed through behaviors such as lack of emotional expression, bragging, and an expansive or inflating posture.

The observations were then mapped to the senators' influence. Positive influence meant that the senators later successfully collaborated with other members of Congress to cosponsor legislation. Negative or no influence meant that collaboration and cosponsorship was generally unsuccessful. Results were clear. Senators who displayed virtuous behaviors tended to become *more* influential once they assumed a leadership position. Senators who displayed vice showed no additional influence, or perhaps even less influence, once the leadership position was assumed.

The results of this experiment suggest that strong morality and ethics tend to create *increased* influence in the workplace. Let's underscore this point:

Strong morality and ethics tend to increase influence in the workplace.

This lesson can be extended well beyond the political arena, into most (if not all) other industries. Cutthroat behaviors do not generally create success. How, then, does this fit in with the numerous articles that have suggested a large percentage of senior executives exhibit psychopathic traits? Well, while people who exhibit such traits may *rise* to positions of power, their callousness and manipulation do not necessarily lead to success once that power is achieved. Narcissism can lead to overconfidence, which can negatively impact decision making. Ruthlessness and callousness can erode support from colleagues. Manipulation may be consciously or unconsciously detected through body language, tone, and facial expressions—and may ultimately have a negative effect on one's level of influence, collaboration, and positive outcome.

The study of the senators seems consistent with this idea—those who exhibited vices were certainly able to rise to power, but they were less effective once they reached the top. "Less effective" is not winning conditions. While perhaps contrary to conventional wisdom, it turns out that we can actually get more done if we are kind. We can create better outcomes overall if we exhibit high moral standards, strength of character, integrity, and respectability.

Remember my consulting project in the toxic work environment? Some of the most disgraceful people on the teams in that organization were the managers and executives who had risen to positions of power—but ultimately they were let go. While no one knows the specific reasons for the terminations, many supposed they were due to negative work results and output. You see, eventually, no one wanted to work with the toxic people. They couldn't get anything done or move the organization forward in a positive way. (Maybe there is good karma after all.) The idea sticks—cutthroat behaviors like entitlement, narcissism, and emotional detachment generally do not create success.

So what if we concentrated on kindness—not for the reciprocity, not for the payoff, but simply for the sake of being kind? What if we began to do thoughtful things for each other, just to make other people a little happier, a little less stressed, a little more fulfilled? When I complimented the actuary on my team for their hard work on the service station project, I felt happy. When I did small favors for my colleagues or helped them with their work, it made me feel good. But when I started becoming consciously aware of my kindness, an element of manipulation seeped in. Yes, I was still being authentic, but it didn't feel good to me to be "keeping track." Once I began noting my small gifts or favors and deliberately logging them in my own mind, it started to feel like trickery. Was my body language also exhibiting an element of manipulation or trickery? Quite possibly, yes.

So I simply began to uplift others, without necessarily taking notice. This was more about paying it forward, more of a random act of kindness. The payoff for being kind was that it made me feel good. And that was the payoff that mattered. Experts have shown that the act of smiling can actually make a person happy. To me, acts of kindness did the same. It turns out that doing good deeds actually does makes you feel better. It reduces stress, helps you feel happier, and can improve your physical well-being. I felt these benefits, and they, in turn, allowed me to be better at my job. They allowed me to create better workplace solutions.

Acts of kindness don't need to be anything major or time-consuming. Perhaps you provide your colleague with a reference, help, or advice. Maybe you buy your desk mate a coffee when they forget their wallet. You hold the door or help someone to the car when they have a lot to carry. You pay someone a compliment. In fact, going forward, if you think something nice in your head, then make a point of actually sharing your kind thought out loud. As long as it's appropriate and not harassment, why keep that kind thought to yourself? Offer your seat to someone at a crowded event. Help someone meet a deadline or cover a shift, even if it's outside your job description. Write a compliment down and leave it at someone's desk. Say thank-you. Tell someone that they are important to you. Retweet. Like. Share. Essentially, go through your days and your weeks and your *life* being kind to others, without expectation of return. You're not doing this so they'll give something back. Instead, you're doing it because it makes you feel good, and because you are a just and thoughtful and kind person.

Educator and poet Julia Abigail Fletcher Carney wrote in 1845, "Little drops of water . . . make the mighty ocean."[13] And so your drops of goodness add up to an ocean of goodness, and this—this!—is your winning conditions. If you can create a culture of positivity and giving, then that is winning conditions. This culture doesn't *compel* people to give but helps them to *want* to give. And you will find that when you uplift those around you, you all lift up together.

When you uplift those around you, you all lift up together.

Throughout my career, I have always felt so blessed and lucky that I led such outstanding teams. The actuaries on my teams were exceptional. They worked hard. They were loyal and happy and conscientious. And I told them so. And I told everyone else. Everyone knew how outstanding my teams were. And you know what happened? Everyone wanted to be on my team. We were the team to be. And we loved that—we loved each other. We sought to always uplift each other. We had a sense of belonging, a sense of community. We gave to each other authentically and selflessly, with our whole hearts. And because we loved our teammates and our work, we worked harder and better and more efficiently and . . . well, you can see the cycle. As we worked harder and better and together, then we really were outstanding. And then more people wanted to be on this outstanding team. They wanted to work with these exceptional actuaries. It was a cycle of winning, which came from kindness.

You can do this, too.

I've seen too many people operate under the idea that the way to make themselves look better is to make everyone around them look worse. It doesn't work that way. It works the opposite of that way. If you can find a way to genuinely uplift those around you, then you're on your way to winning conditions.

---

13 Hanson, E.R. *Our Woman Workers: Biographical Sketches of Women Eminent in the Universalist Church for Literary, Philanthropic and Christian Work.* 1881.

CONSIDER YOUR EXTENDED NETWORK

I shared with you some examples of the atmosphere of giving on my teams, but please don't assume that our immediate teams are the only colleagues that deserve our kindness. Think about your full network of people, including internal teams, peers, and higher-ups. Think about external business partners like vendors, regulators, and consultants. Think about your customers—past, current, and future. Think about your building's extended staff, like janitors, cafeteria servers, and elevator operators. Think about your communities outside the workplace—your friends, family members, neighbors. All of these people deserve our kindness.

How often have you walked past your organization's security staff without saying good morning or asking their names? How often have you paid for your lunch without smiling at the cashier? At one former organization, people nicknamed me the Elevator Concierge. Every time I got in the elevator, it seemed I knew someone or met someone. It was easy—because it was simple kindness. My friend Debra and I knew everyone at Penn, and this is probably why I won that election in college and kicked off my entire quest toward winning conditions over thirty years ago. This was all borne from love and kindness.

Perhaps the manipulative pregivers focus only on higher-ups or customers who can provide a "useful" return. But selfless giving and a community spirit applies to many different connections. Remember that we all have so much to offer each other, and developing positive relationships in and out of the workplace enables the entire collective network to benefit. Consider that the most optimal network of connections will push your limits of capability, thinking, and expression. A network like this will promote and enhance your engagement and happiness in and out of your work role. Your network will inspire innovation and help to provide a sense of purpose. So respect others. Give them dignity. It doesn't matter if they are the CEO or the intern. Sometimes something huge springs unexpectedly from a simple act of kindness.

About a year ago, a leader from a professional education company emailed me out of the blue to ask if I would create and present an online educational webinar on a technical topic. Apparently there were some open sessions in the event calendar, and they wanted to engage some new presenters. At the time, I was completely swamped. My season of *Survivor* had just aired, and speaking requests were coming in fast and furious. I had been elected to the board of my professional society, and we had a great deal of important work to complete for our members. I was traveling a lot. My kids were growing up, and I didn't want to miss any of their school events or sports games. I was volunteering in my community and for my alma mater. Time was tight. But honestly, they seemed like the nicest person ever, and I kind of just wanted to do them this favor— even though I'd never met or spoken with them before. I'm guessing that whatever they wrote to compel me to do this motivated me in exactly the way I needed to be motivated.

So I agreed to the webinar. And then the work began. Over many late nights, I slogged through the slide deck. I secretly complained to my husband that I had taken on too much: "Remind me not to do this again! What was I thinking?!" But despite my complaints, it felt good to help out a virtual stranger. Despite missing out on some sleep, the relationship was fruitful. The webinar was a huge success, pulling in a large number of listeners who provided extremely positive feedback for both my presentation and the education company overall.

About six months after we recorded the webinar, the same leader from the same professional education company reached out again. They had another open slot. They kindly asked me if I'd consider preparing and delivering another learning webinar, this time on communication techniques. I thoughtfully considered the request. But I also considered my red marbles. I needed time to add red marbles to my urn. At this time I was concentrating on finishing my book, and I was poised to begin the arduous process of finding a literary agent. Finding a literary agent can be a massive undertaking, so I needed to seriously limit my side gigs if I were going to embark on that process.

Now, for those of you who aren't aware of the process for publishing a book through traditional channels, here's how it happens. First, you write your book. Then you pitch your book to literary agents through a process known as *querying.* Your literary agent is the person who will pitch your book to the publishing houses, so if you want a traditional publishing deal, then you will probably need an agent. Querying literary agents means researching thousands of agents and then sending personalized letters, sample chapters, author background, market comparisons, and other information to those agents who may be the right fit for your book. You do this until one or more agents decides to offer you representation. The querying process can take weeks, months, or years. Authors may query a handful or hundreds of agents and may quickly or never be offered representation. Clearly, the process of securing a literary agent can be extremely time-consuming. And so I kindly declined the second webinar with the truthful reason why: I was about to begin looking for an agent. This book was important to me. I'd love to help them out another time, but I wasn't able to do this one.

Their response: "My mother is a literary agent. If you send me your book, I'll ask her to provide some feedback."

I COULD NOT BELIEVE THIS. I sent the book off on a Thursday night, and she replied by Monday. She was incredible—she read my work in a weekend and provided great feedback. Having been enriched by her advice and perspective, I ended up finding and signing with my literary agent in FOUR DAYS.

This gave me plenty of time to do the second webinar—which of course I did happily. We had both done something just to be kind. Neither of us was looking for a payoff. And we both won.

It's win-winning conditions!

FINDING THE GOODNESS IN PEOPLE

I've provided some examples for ways that you can show kindness in the workplace. Some were action based—like writing a referral, covering a shift, or creating and delivering a webinar for a complete stranger to help fill an empty calendar slot. Some were verbal—like paying a compliment or telling someone that they and their contributions are valuable. Even though the verbal acts of kindness may be quick and easy (no late-night slog!), they can still be quite impactful. Consider this.

During college, a friend of mine began volunteering at a local wildlife rehabilitation facility. His responsibilities included feeding, cleaning, and caring for injured or abandoned animals, with the goal of safely rereleasing the wildlife back into their natural environments. About a year into his volunteer position, a staff position opened up, and a professional rehabilitator joined the team. The rehabilitator had a great deal of knowledge about animals and their care, but they weren't the easiest personality to get along with. Okay, they were downright difficult. The rehabilitator criticized the volunteers liberally and often, insinuating that they didn't really know much, they weren't smart, and they weren't doing a good job. Many of the volunteers requested to not work during that rehabilitator's shifts, because they were so difficult, negative, and disruptive.

I remember my friend telling me this story, and I asked him how he felt about his volunteer position given the constant negativity. It turns out, he was no longer a target of the rehabilitator's disapproval. Because one day, he consciously decided to try a new tactic—kindness. My friend would say, "You have so much rich knowledge, can you tell me how you learned about all this?" or "Can you teach me how to do this? I want to learn to do it like you do." And he meant it. The curious thing was that as he continued sharing kindness, he eventually got kindness back. The rehabilitator softened and began openly sharing their knowledge. They stopped making those digs at every turn. And the volunteers—all of them—ended up learning a lot. They learned new ways to handle the animals and how to deliver the very best care.

It turns out that finding the goodness not only in ourselves—but also in *other* people—is winning conditions. I'm guessing that we can all think of people we've worked with who have been difficult. Perhaps they focus on negativity constantly, insult us, or otherwise consistently treat us poorly. Is it possible to share acts of kindness with these difficult employees? I know this isn't possible with everyone (I've already shared my own stories of toxic people that I was not able to convert to kindness), but it's sure worth a try. Can we work to create a positive chemistry with as many people as possible? Can we create an entire aura of positivity?

By choosing goodness and kindness over cutthroat and negative behaviors, we can create a greater likelihood of success. Remember that sometimes our greatest successes come from the small things that add up over time. The little drops of water create the mighty ocean. The days when you connect with someone positively all do lead to a greater story—the winning story. Your winning story.

Remember that we don't need to be entirely altruistic and *always* put others' needs in front of our own. Back in Chapter 8, we learned that self-care means securing your own oxygen mask first. You shouldn't have to feel as if you need to give every single ounce of yourself and your time to others. It's also okay to set boundaries, and it's okay to say no when you're protecting your own red marbles. But beyond that, we can do good for others. We can enjoy our work and create an environment in which we *want* to go to work—and in which our colleagues *want* to work with us. We can help to make our workplaces more pleasant and lift everyone up together.

Build a résumé of positivity. Have compassion. Have empathy. Have integrity. Be kind. Be good. Be thoughtful. Be the Amazing You.

YOUR WINNING STORY

I wasn't born a winner. There was a time when I felt like everything I tried, I came up just short of success. But I was determined to be something. And so I became consciously aware of the details that mattered.

I looked outward. I began to probe deeper in order to better discover, anticipate, and address my colleagues' responses, motivations, and concerns. I sought to understand how past events might impact my current interactions. I learned to build a coalition of advocates who would support my work and my success. I recognized that people view situations from different perspectives, and accommodating their perspectives led to better outcomes. I practiced changing my language based on the needs of my audiences. I opened my eyes to their current levels of contentment so that I could better understand and articulate the impact of my great work. I became more mindful of decision bias, so that neither I nor my business partners made decisions that left us in a suboptimal state.

But I also looked inward. I recognized that I needed to create my own great experiences in order to create more opportunity for growth. So I persisted in taking steps toward my goals, concentrating on adding red marbles to my urn. I learned how to define and share my own value so that others could learn about the many fine qualities I had to offer. I practiced strengthening my magnetism, because I had learned that when people want to be around you, they will want to work with you. They will want you to succeed.

All of this I did with great love, and kindness, and integrity, and respect.

Twenty-five years after launching the winning conditions framework, I found myself at the top of my career. My work and my contributions to my profession had been celebrated through television, internet, and print media. I was named a pioneer and trailblazer in my industry. I was admitted to one of the top educational institutions in the US and elected to the board of directors of one of the most prestigious professional associations globally. I guest lectured at top universities. For all intents and purposes, I was a winner.

But I didn't yet feel like a winner. Why not? What was I missing?

I had thought I'd put all the pieces together to build my masterpiece, but it turns out that my puzzle wasn't complete. There was still a hole. There was a piece missing. It took a swimming race against a marine for me to find that last piece—the piece that I needed to feel like my story was a winning story.

DIVING IN

Once I lived outside on a beach in Fiji for almost six weeks straight. There was clean water to drink, but no clean water in which to wash, so I didn't wash my hair or brush my teeth for those entire six weeks. I didn't even have a change of clothes. I know this sounds awful, but it was oddly refreshing to not worry about clothes, or makeup, or appearances. There wasn't any technology, or even electricity, no Instagram or Facebook or Twitter to distract me. There also wasn't much to eat on that island, so cooking wasn't really an issue. A little rice, a little fish, maybe a small sip of sweet coconut water. My stomach stopped growling after about a week, though, so the lack of food felt manageable. The biggest part of meal prep involved picking giant leaves out of the trees to use as plates. I washed them. Washing leaves—sounds very rustic and simple and maybe even idyllic, doesn't it?

Except that it wasn't so simple. Because I lived on that island with seventeen strangers, and we played psychological war games. At every moment. We strategized, we planned, we aligned. We manipulated and we schemed. We blindsided and were blindsided. We competed with and against each other, voting each other off that idyllic island one by one over thirty-nine days. We played relentlessly to be the last remaining player on the island, the sole survivor. Because that last one standing walks away with $1 million.

For sixteen years I had applied to do this thing—to live simply on that idyllic island and play extreme psychological war games. Ah, the adventure! One might think I would be fully prepared after all that time. And this is somewhat true. There were only about four weeks between my invitation to play and my departure, and I used those four weeks wisely. I joined a pool and swam laps every day. Ten laps, twenty laps, fifty laps. Eventually I just swam laps until I got bored. I practiced diving and holding my breath. I practiced balance and agility. I stretched. I lifted weights. I ran. Okay, I walked, because my knees aren't great (and I'm lazy), but in my head it was running. I mastered slide puzzles and tangrams. I binged prior seasons of the show to study challenges, camp life, and relationships. I weaned myself off coffee and gained some weight. I got my vaccines. I requested an unpaid leave of absence from my work that I loved, and was promptly fired, but it didn't matter to me, because I was headed out to live a dream. I prepared my family, prepaid the bills that were due while I was gone, and I said my goodbyes. I was ready—I had put all the pieces together to build my masterpiece! This puzzle was complete!

But then, it seemed, it wasn't. I had prepared for the game like I had prepared for my career successes—with thoughtful, mindful, and directed planning and execution. I knew what I wanted and went after it. I considered all the details. But then, the very first minute of the game, I saw there was a hole. Apparently I wasn't actually ready after all. I had spent sixteen years working on this puzzle, but this was no masterpiece.

I remember landing on the beach and learning that I was playing this game with a group of heroes—a firefighter, an Olympian, a marine, an ocean rescue lifeguard, and an NFL player. I was an actuary and a mom, and I had absolutely no idea why I was there. I had no elevator speech for this group. I could find no similarities. I couldn't articulate any reason that I belonged with a group of heroes. I pretended I did—I think I even said that I felt like a hero, but that was a lie—a lie I told myself and a lie I told the others. Maybe in some way I thought that if I said it enough, I could make it true. But I didn't feel at all like a hero. Instead, I felt like a fraud. I felt horrible that the producers had picked me to play, because soon they'd find out that they'd made a big mistake.

My tribe of heroes thought I was a fraud, too. They didn't think I belonged with them. They saw that I was an older mom and not a hero and thought I'd lose challenges, and they wanted to keep the group strong. They nicknamed me Mom Squad and decided to vote me out of their group—and out of the game. And so, despite my preparation, despite my swimming and walking and puzzling and balancing, despite my planning sixteen years to live this dream, despite all this great preparation, a doubt creeped in and took hold. And after that, I couldn't see the dream. I could only see the hole.

I've mentioned that after the first challenge I became physically sick (yes, I'm the one who vomited on primetime television in front of ten million people), and people often ask me why that happened. The truth? I was so terrified, and I felt so out of place, and I knew that the producers had made a big mistake with me. This was bigger than my fear of public speaking or fear of starting graduate school. This was a global Doubt. My body physically reacted, and I couldn't stop it. You see, this thing called Doubt is a powerful thing. It can seep into your soul and eat through every ounce of your preparation. In an instant, it can inflict amnesia, making you forget all of your good and worthy and impressive achievements. You can look outward and inward all you want, but this Doubt is the killer of success. Doubt steals that last puzzle piece and leaves that gaping hole. Doubt had not been invited in, but it barged in nonetheless. It got in my head and mocked me. It told me I was a fool for thinking I could do this.

And so, instead of living my dream, I found myself just trying to get through it. Every day became a day I just needed to get through. What a terrible way to live a dream, isn't it? Just trying to get through it. This is also a terrible way to live your life. I had set up my winning conditions, but the uninvited Doubt stained them. The uninvited Doubt teased that I'm not so good today. I don't fit in today. I'm not a winner today. This is no winning story.

To counter this, I began the waiting game. I just waited. Waited for tomorrow. Anything to get through today. Because tomorrow is my day. Yes, tomorrow. Always tomorrow. If I can just make it to tomorrow, then tomorrow I'll fit in. Tomorrow I'll feel better. Tomorrow I'll shake this doubt. Tomorrow I will succeed. Tomorrow is my day. I'm not so good today, but you just wait and see what I can be tomorrow. TOMORROW I WILL BE A WINNER!

Have you ever felt this way? Have you ever felt like you just need to pass today so you can make it to tomorrow?

> Tomorrow I'll get a promotion.

> Tomorrow I'll get a raise.

> Tomorrow I'll be better at XYZ.

> Tomorrow I'll know more, learn more, have more.

> Tomorrow they will see me.

> Tomorrow they will recognize me.

> Tomorrow I'll get up and do it.

▸ Tomorrow I'll be more productive.

▸ Tomorrow I'll be successful.

If you've ever felt this way, then you're not so different from me. Ah, Tomorrow. The curious thing about Tomorrow is that it never actually gets here. Tomorrow is a perpetual no-show. And when the uninvited Doubt teams up with its pal No-Show Tomorrow, the two become doubly compelling. So here I am after sixteen years, plagued by Doubt, waiting for Tomorrow, waiting, waiting—well, it made me wonder what happened to all of my beautiful preparation. What had happened to my confidence and my success? Where were my winning conditions? I had worked so long and so hard, crossed those t's and dotted those i's. But there was still something missing. The uninvited Doubt and No-Show Tomorrow plagued me for weeks. They followed me constantly, making sure I felt not good enough. Not strong enough. Not fast enough. Not young enough. Not cool enough. Not anything enough. Just. Not. Enough.

Do you ever feel like you just aren't enough?

Thirty years ago, when I was a junior in college, I experienced a distinctly pivotal moment that changed my life. I won an election that moved me toward a lifetime of winning conditions. After more than three weeks on that idyllic island, I experienced another pivotal moment—a moment that turned the winning conditions into a winning story.

On day twenty-two, there were only ten of us left in the game, and we were competing in a challenge for a feast on a yacht. The lack of food over the first three weeks of the game had left us wasting away. We needed that feast, and we needed it desperately. My part of the challenge would begin on a dock anchored somewhere out in the South Pacific Ocean. I needed to dive off my dock, swim out to a second dock, climb up a very tall ladder, jump off that tall ladder into the ocean below, and then swim to a buoy. Once at the buoy, I'd dive down underwater and untie a set of keys and then swim the keys to a third dock. And apparently I needed to do all this while RACING AGAINST A MARINE.

The marine was an incredible man, a true hero, a fierce competitor, and more than a decade younger than me. I was not a marine. I was a forty-six-year-old mom and actuary, and today was not my day. Tomorrow was my day.

▸ I can't swim so fast today.

▸ I can't dive today.

▸ I can't untie keys very quickly today.

▸ I'm going to make a fool of myself today.

▸ I'm going to lose the challenge for my team today.

▸ We won't have a feast on a yacht today.

▸ We won't eat again today.

▸ We won't win because of me today.

▸ I can't beat that marine today.

Maybe tomorrow. Tomorrow is my day.

And so I began freaking out on the dock. But then . . . my moment. I was standing on that dock, anchored somewhere out in the South Pacific Ocean, with a beautiful and good firefighter. That beautiful and good firefighter saw that I was panicked and struggling. He looked over at me and very calmly said, "Chrissy, just hold your mask, dive in, and swim your little heart out."

Just dive in and swim your little heart out.

He was telling me more than what to do. He was telling me that I was already enough. It didn't matter if I beat the marine. It didn't matter how fast I swam. Or how well I dived. Or if I untied the keys first. Or if we won the feast. All that mattered was that I swam my little heart out. You see, it turns out that I was already enough. It was the piece I hadn't seen. For minutes, weeks, years. And then I discovered it. It had been there all along.

So guess what I did?

I held my mask, I dived in, and I swam my little heart out. I swam to the dock and I climbed up the giant ladder and I jumped into the ocean below and I swam to the buoy and I untied the keys and when I came up for air I heard the doctor screaming, "Chrissy, you're winning! Chrissy, you're winning!" and yes, I won my swimming leg against the marine, and our team won the feast on the yacht that day.

That race was a turning point in my game, when my game of tomorrows became a game of todays. When I finally felt like enough, then I was. I just needed a little help finding that last piece. I learned that tomorrow is *not* my day. Nope, I do not need to wait for Tomorrow. It turns out that *Today* is my day. Let me shout it! TODAY IS MY DAY! TODAY IS MY DAY!

After I found Today, I went on to win four individual chal-

With host Jeff Probst after winning individual immunity in *Survivor*, season 35, episode 11: 'Buy One, Get One Free." Image courtesy of CBS.

lenges and tie a record for the most individual immunity wins by a woman in the game's history. I lasted thirty-nine days in that game and came in second place. No, it wasn't first place, but this was a huge win for me! I was supposed to be the first one out; instead, I made it to day thirty-nine. I came out of the game with millions of viewers rooting for me. There were articles, webcasts, and podcasts in support of my game published across media channels throughout the world. Something had resonated. I had been an underdog—the Mom Squad on a tribe of heroes. But it turned out, I was a hero, too. It turned out, those producers knew exactly what they were doing when they picked me. They didn't make a big mistake. Instead, they saw something in me that I hadn't seen in myself.

Sometimes people see things in us that we don't see in ourselves. We all have greatness within us. You are not a fraud. It's what I've been telling you from the beginning—you are outstanding. You are exceptional. You are motivated and dedicated. Your choices and opinions are valid and valuable. Let yourself see and feel the extraordinary greatness that is you.

When I reflect on my *Survivor* game, I think a lot about my difference in performance before and after day twenty-two. I had the same preparation and ability before and after day twenty-two, so what changed and enabled me to begin to win? It was the last piece of the winning conditions. I needed to not just live it, but I needed to *feel* it. I needed to believe in myself. I needed to believe that I had a winning story. When I finally felt like enough, well, then I was.

YOU ARE ENOUGH

After the game was over, the producers gave me a stack of letters that my family had written to me while I was in the game. They are the most beautiful love letters. I read them still, to remind myself that I am enough. My sister Sandra wrote me one of those letters. She wrote (shortened for brevity):

Dear Chrissy,

I knew it! I just knew it! I knew one day you'd get your buff—you are so buff-worthy! I'm so proud of you!!!

I've written this letter to you a thousand times in the wee hours of the morning and late at night, so you know you are always in my thoughts, and I'm saying a prayer for you every day. But I know you don't need it. If there is anyone, ANYONE who is prepared for this, it's you.

Use every life lesson and skill you have and keep going, Chrissy, and most of all, have fun doing it! So outwit, outplay, and outlast the competition. I know you can and you will. And remember—in life there are limits, but they only apply to other people.

I love you. Love, San

My sister wrote this letter to me, but it applies to all of us. It's a love letter to all of us:

You are worthy. I am proud of you. If there is anyone, ANYONE who is prepared for this, it's you. Use these winning conditions and keep going. Have fun doing it. I know you can and you will. In life there are limits, but they only apply to other people.

You are enough.

And perhaps this is the most important lesson of all. Stretch. Grow. Help others. Smile. Look outward. Look inward. But above all else, believe in yourself. Believe in your own winning story. You have a winning story. And I can't wait to read it.

ACKNOWLEDGMENTS

They say it takes a village to raise a child, and I've learned it's not so different with publishing a book. So many incredible people have made this book possible, and I am so grateful that you all are in my world. YOU are my Winning Conditions.

Thank you to my incredible editor Hannah Bennett, who helped turn my caterpillar into a butterfly. You taught me so much as we worked together on this project, and I can't imagine having done this with anyone else. Thank you to my rock star agent Jessica Faust, who took a chance on me, taught me about flow and a million other things, and answered all of my important (and sometimes ridiculous) questions with enthusiasm and support.

I wouldn't have even made it to the agent stage without my three biggest cheerleaders—my mom Christine Lewis and my sisters Ellen Bates and Sandra Muller. Thank you for reading multiple rounds of drafts and conference calling every other week to share your feedback. But mostly, thanks for the notes you'd send out of the blue, sharing your enthusiasm over the winning conditions you were already implementing daily in your own lives. It was your real-life success stories that made me believe these ideas were important enough to share, and easy enough to execute. Thank you to my friends Suzanne Andrews and Carol Navin, who read shells of early drafts and helped focus my ideas and language with encouragement and excitement.

Thank you to Megan Rosen, Cassandra Dunn, and Dr. Timothy Coomer, who selflessly shared their time and expertise helping me understand the agenting and publishing process. It was a chance encounter meeting Tim in an airport that tipped the first domino. "You should write a book," he said. And I did. Good thing I had my elevator speech ready that time.

ACKNOWLEDGMENTS

Thank you to all of the incredible people I've met throughout my career, my travels, my studies, and my volunteerism, who illuminated the various pieces of winning conditions. Each of you taught me some lesson along the way. While many of you have remained anonymous within these pages, I'd like to give special thanks to those whom I celebrated by name—my still remarkable and still best friend Holly Stark Gilbert; my forever college biddie Debra Laboschin (I think we really did know the entire school); the amazing Roselyn Feinsod, who taught me far more than the power of a gracious thank you; Holly Schmidt, who continues to always ask the right questions to develop the best solutions (and always with joy and a smile).

Thank you to Christine Lewis, who brilliantly built not only a company, but a family, within her organization; Suzanne Andrews, who I'd often watch with awe, as she gracefully and diplomatically handled some of the most complex and difficult situations and personalities; my former managers Linda O'Brien and Frank (a pseudonym, you know who you are), who not only taught me how to deliver my work, but also created a working environment that enabled me to thrive—I loved learning so much from both of you; my beautiful and now grown-up children, Andrew, Mike, and Elise Hofbeck, who lovingly filmed and edited my *Survivor* audition videos, always with endless support and excitement over their mom's crazy dream (and yes, Andrew scored an incredible internship!).

Thank you to David Herzog, the CFO who after our unlikely meeting (twice!) in an elevator, gave me yet another chance to better introduce myself when we rode the ferry together months later; Ellen Bates, an incredible labor and delivery nurse who was a gift to her patients, and inspires me every day; and Sandra Muller, who not only believed I'd one day get my buff, but has always championed all of my dreams—I believe in you, and yours, too. While unnamed in this book, I'd also like to thank JP Hilsabeck, the firefighter who assured me I could just dive in and swim my little heart out. I will always be deeply grateful to you all.

And finally, thank you to my incredible family—my husband Keith, and my Andrew, Mike, and Elise. You have shown me nothing but endless love. I love you all beyond words. You are always winners to me.

ABOUT THE AUTHOR

Christine Hofbeck is a consulting actuary, progressing from individual contributor to executive advisor for several massive and influential global organizations. She's an in-demand keynote speaker and holds degrees from both the University of Pennsylvania and MIT. In 2017 Christine (Chrissy) competed on CBS's hit reality television show *Survivor*. She's traveled through all seven continents and enjoyed some moments of insanity through skydiving, hang gliding, and a polar plunge in Antarctica. Christine lives in New Jersey with her husband Keith, kids Andrew, Mike, and Elise, and two crazy cats.